What Goes on in Momma's Closet

Bonita Townsend

What Goes on in Momma's Closet

Momma's Closet

TATE PUBLISHING
AND ENTERPRISES, LLC

What Goes On In Momma's Closet
Copyright © 2016 by Bonita Townsend. All rights reserved.

No part of this publication may be reproduced, stored in a retrieval system or transmitted in any way by any means, electronic, mechanical, photocopy, recording or otherwise without the prior permission of the author except as provided by USA copyright law.

This book is designed to provide accurate and authoritative information with regard to the subject matter covered. This information is given with the understanding that neither the author nor Tate Publishing, LLC is engaged in rendering legal, professional advice. Since the details of your situation are fact dependent, you should additionally seek the services of a competent professional.

The opinions expressed by the author are not necessarily those of Tate Publishing, LLC.

Published by Tate Publishing & Enterprises, LLC
127 E. Trade Center Terrace | Mustang, Oklahoma 73064 USA
1.888.361.9473 | www.tatepublishing.com

Tate Publishing is committed to excellence in the publishing industry. The company reflects the philosophy established by the founders, based on Psalm 68:11,

"The Lord gave the word and great was the company of those who published it."

Book design copyright © 2016 by Tate Publishing, LLC. All rights reserved.
Cover design by Junriel Boquecosa
Interior design by Manolito Bastasa

Published in the United States of America

ISBN: 978-1-63418-811-1
1. Biography & Autobiography / Personal Memoirs
2. Religion / Christian Life / Prayer
16.02.19

In remembrance of my daddy
John Allen Hildreth…

My books:

Sleeping With the Beast
Mommas 911 Prayers
Mommas Life Tips

My next books:

"God Really Works, thru Em Ole Maids,"
and "In and Out the Closet."
It talks about how God works through
the faith of some ole' maids.
It tells you about God powers.
It shows us that God can use anybody.
It talks about my painful childhood.
It talks about so called Christians.
It talks about how God can bring the dead back.
It tells about God healing powerful addictions.
It has healing powerful prayers.

Do not forget to get your copy about how God heals and deliverers. He is real and very much alive. He lives in us today.

—"Mommas' Closet Journal," 7Heaven Inc.

God says that the more hopeless your circumstances, the more likely your salvation.

The greater your cares, the more genuine your prayers will be.

The darker the room, the greater the need for light

God's help is near and always available, but it is only given to those who seek it.

Faith is the belief that God will do what is right.

Introduction

This book was written with a heart to help and encourage God's people wherever they may be and whatever situation they may find themselves in. Let us face it, at some time or another we are all confronted with challenging obstacles. However, we must realize that it is not our own strength that will pull us along in life. One objective of this book is to look at the lives of some of the men and women of the Bible, many of whom were ordinary people just like you and me, and see the insurmountable obstacles they faced and how their faith in God brought them through to victory every time! These were people who had every opportunity to quit at times when everything seemed to be against them. These were not necessarily great men and women but they were men and women with great faith in a great God. By looking at their lives and the tests and trials they faced we can learn valuable lessons from them for our own, "fight of faith" in the day and hour in which we live. God's people should hold on to God's Words in every trying circumstance and in every difficult situation, no matter how impossible it may look. This is the only way to be successful in life. God will always make a way for us! In addition, God's message to us is still the same today as it has always been. "Don't Quit! Keep trusting me. Your faith in Me will see you through!"

Today I am praying that God touch each one of us today. I pray that we will be able to bring good fruit forth. Father God, Your Word is my compass and it helps me to see my life as complete in Jesus Christ. I cast all my cares away and rely on You, that I might be well balanced, vigilant and cautious at all times. Amen.

As you are obedient to God and rely on the power of the Spirit, you will experience the daily reality of your heavenly blessings in Christ as they manifest themselves in God's:

> PEACE in your life circumstances,
> LOVE that is unconditional and constant,
> FAITH that is strong and unwavering, and
> GRACE along with continued blessings.

Stay blessed in the Lord with all spiritual blessings.

Father God, I thank You that You have blessed me with all spiritual blessings in Christ Jesus. Through skillful and godly wisdom is my house (my family) built, and by understanding it is established on a sound foundation. In addition, by knowledge its chambers shall be filled with priceless treasure. The house of the uncompromisingly righteous shall stand. Prosperity and welfare are in my house, in the name of Jesus. Father God, as for me my house, we will serve the Lord, in Jesus' name. Hallelujah! Amen.

Section 1

1

GOD'S POWER IS AMAZING

When I was around six years old, my Momma Juanita and I were listening to James Brown. We were listening to the Big Pay Back. We were singing and mixing up all the words in the songs we heard. James Brown would have been so disappointed. I'll never forget how Momma was laughing at me. She told me that I didn't dance like a colored girl. We looked like two drunken people singing and dancing. We both laughed about it but that still didn't stop me from dancing though.

Next thing I knew, we heard a loud, continuous, thumping noise. Then the sound got louder.

[Knock-Knock-Knock]

I yelled, "Momma, someone is at the door!"

[Bump-Bam-Bam]

The knocking continued and got louder and louder.

Momma cut off the music and went to the door. She peeped out the window that was mounted on the door. Before she could open the door, we heard someone yell, "Ms. Juanita! Please open up your door! Please help me!"

Momma looked down at me and said, "I don't know if I need to open this door."

I asked "Why not?"

Momma said, "Because it's a white lady at my door with blood on her. They might think that I did something to her. They would hang me from the biggest tree that they could find."

The lady said, "I know you see me at this door. Your music stopped playing. Please open up! Please help me Ms. Juanita!" She knocked on the door again and said, "I am not going anywhere until you open up this door."

"Okay," Momma replied as she began to open it. "Come in," Momma said. The lady walked inside and somewhat introduced herself.

"Hello, I am Mrs. Smith. I heard that you can bring dead people back to life. Why didn't you want to open the door up for me?"

Momma answered her, "Because we still live in the seventies and if someone had seen you at my door with all that blood on you then what do you think other people would have thought? Just think about it. There is a white woman standing at our door in an all-black neighborhood with blood all over her."

The only time that a white person came to the door of a black person during that time was to pick up a black person to go to work.

There in our front room stood a tall, slim, white lady. Mrs. Smith was as white as a ghost. She was shaking and big crocodile teardrops were falling from her eyes. She was covered in blood. It was all over her white blouse.

Momma asked Mrs. Smith, "Are you okay? Because you're bleeding."

Mrs. Smith said, "It's not my blood; it's my son Jimmy's blood."

She continued, "Jimmy was riding on his motorcycle and he was hit by a drunken driver. Dr. Johnson said for me to go make funeral arrangements because he had lost entirely too much blood and he has a brain concussion. It's just no way he's going to make it throughout the night. Ms. Juanita, I don't know where to turn to or what to do. I need you." She hesitated but then went on to cry, "I heard that you can bring people back from the state of death. Please Ms. Juanita! Help me and my son before he dies. They told me that he's going to die! Please help me! I will do anything. I have money. I'll pay you at whatever the cost. Just please keep him from dying. I need you!"

Momma grabbed Mrs. Smith and said, "First I need you to go to the bathroom and clean yourself up. While you are bathing, I'll find you some fresh clean clothes to put on."

Mrs. Smith asked, "What about Jimmy?"

Momma told her that she needed the shirt that she had on because it had Jimmy's blood on it. Mrs. Smith went into the bathroom and turned on the shower. We still could hear her crying over the shower water. She stayed in there about twenty minutes. Finally, she turned off the water and stepped out of the shower. Momma was waiting with a nice, warm towel and some fresh, clean clothes for her to put on. She asked her to meet her in the living room once she was finished getting dressed.

Mrs. Smith entered the living room and sat down on the couch.

She said, "You must think that I am crazy."

"No! I don't think that," Momma replied.

Then Mrs. Smith said, "I don't know why not. I'm a random white woman coming to your door demanding that you bring my son back from the dead. I know…I know, I guess I'm just pretty darn desperate."

"I can't bring dead people back to life," Momma proclaimed. "That's God's job. Now, I will be glad to pray with you. Is that something you want me to do with you?"

Mrs. Smith nodded her head agreeing to pray with Momma. Momma then lit up one white, blue, and gold candle then two red ones. At that moment, she asked God to forgive them of all of their sins.

> Our Father which art in heaven, it is written in Your Word that if I confess with my mouth that Jesus is the Lord and believe in my heart that you have raised Him from the dead, I shall be saved. Therefore, Father, I confess that Jesus is my Lord. I make Him Lord of my life right now. I believe in my heart that you raised Jesus from the dead. I renounce my past life with Satan and close the door to his devices. I thank you for forgiving me of all my sins. Jesus is my Lord, I am a new creation. Old things have passed away and now all things become new in the name of Jesus Christ, Amen.

> She started reading Psalm 51.
> Have mercy upon me, O God, according to thy loving-kindness: according unto the multitude of thy tender mercies blot out my transgressions. Wash me thoroughly from mine iniquity, and cleanse me from my sin. For I acknowledge my transgressions. Against You, You only, have I sinned, and done this evil in Your sight–that You may be found just when

You speak, and blameless when you judge. Behold, I was sharpening in iniquity and in sin did my Momma conceive me. Behold, thou desirest truth in the inward parts; and in hidden part thou shalt make me to know wisdom. Purge me with hyssop, and I shall be clean; wash me, and I shall be whiter that snow. Make me hear joy and gladness that the bones you have broken may rejoice. Hide Your face from my sins, and blot out all my iniquities. Create in me a clean heart, O God, And renew a steadfast spirit within me. Do not cast me away from your presence. And do not take Your Holy Spirit from me. Restore to me the joy of your salvation. And uphold me by your generous Spirit. Then I will teach transgressors your ways. And sinners shall be converted to you. Deliver me from the guilt of bloodshed, O God, the God of my salvation, and my tongue shall sing aloud of your righteousness. O Lord, open my lips, and my mouth shall show forth praise. For do not desire Sacrifice or else I would have given it. You do not delight in burnt offerings. The sacrifices of God are a broken spirit, a broken a contrite heart–these, O God, You will not despise, Do well in pleasure to Zion. Build the walls of Jerusalem. Then you shall be pleased with the sacrifices of the righteousness. With burnt offerings and whole burnt offerings; then they shall offer bulls on your altar.

Then Momma got down on her knees and asked Mrs. Smith to join her. Momma started talking to God on Mrs. Smith's behalf then Mrs. Smith joined in with her. They stayed on their knees for quite a long time. In amazement, Momma stood up and began speaking in tongues. At that moment, I recalled the room going dark. It was so murky that you could not see anything. Both the women were quiet. You could hear a pin fall if one had dropped. It seemed that the room stayed dark for a long time. Then all of a sudden the light came back on. It was so bright seeing all of the colorful lights in the air. They were everywhere in the room. I cannot explain it but I will try to the best of my ability. I remember feeling at peace. I knew as long as I stayed in the room there was nothing that could harm me. I felt completely safe from everything evil. I recognized that this had to be the spirit of the Lord. Nothing could touch me! God's aura was everywhere. His healing powers were there in that room. Momma trusted God to do what He said He would do. Her faith was so strong in God that she had the power to intervene in other people's prayers. God heard her every time she prayed for other people.

Mrs. Smith jumped up off her knees and proclaimed, "Jimmy, baby, I know that you're okay, honey. Thank you

Lord, my God. Thank you Jesus! Jimmy is not going to die. He's going to live." She cried tears of happiness to Momma.

Then she said, "Ms. Juanita, I know that you don't have the power to bring people back from the dead, but I do know that God does hear your prayers. I am so glad you opened your door for me. I thank you for allowing God to work through you. Jimmy is okay now. How much do I owe you Ms. Juanita?"

With a smile, Momma humbly replied, "Nothing."

Mrs. Smith gave her some money anyway and said, "Thanks for your time… Oh, and for the clean clothes too. I need to get back to the hospital to be with my son before he wakes up." That is exactly what I remember. She walked out of the front door singing and still giving God praises. I will never forget that moment in my childhood.

Some of Momma's family members told her that she had made a mistake for praying to get a new house and to have her cleaning business. She was told that she was not mentally stable enough to have a new house and run a business. Momma was more strong-minded than what people gave her credit for, and she did not listen to all of that outside, negative influence. She believed that if she prayed about it then God would handle the rest. He always seemed to do just that. Despite everyone else's doubt, she opened up her new business and built a new brick house on Lincoln Drive. That is where she ran her cleaning service. At one point, she wondered if everyone else had been right about her making a big mistake, because she was not getting any feedback from any potential customers. With the new house and the business sitting at bay, eventually her phone started ringing. People were looking for Momma to clean their house and some were even still talking about Jimmy.

We lived in a small town called Camden, Arkansas and the word didn't take long to spread about Momma's faith and the connection she had with God. Some of her clients hired her to clean their house but that's not what she was asked to do once she got there. Most of them wanted her to pray for them and their family members. She was not just cleaning houses; she was also there to clean out the bad forces of this world. Before she knew it, she was super busy. She was making unbelievable money. God opened up a money-well for her. He opened doors that were supposed to be closed. Her faith was amazing. The faith that she had was big enough to carry another person along.

She earned many different names in our small town. They were names like "God's Child" to even more unpleasant ones such as "Witch Doctor." Not only did she earn her fair share of names, so did my brother Herman and I. I used to run home from the bus stop in tears because of the children from my school. They called me "Witchie Poo Girl" and I was harassed on a daily basis. For example,

I remember some of the kids would say stuff like, "Let us see you bring back this dead frog" or it would be whatever dead animal/insect in sight. The other children were talking about how nasty my Momma was because she cleaned houses for a living.

I remember my Momma overheard me crying one day and she asked me, "What's wrong with you Maria? Why are you crying?" I did not want to tell her but my heart felt like it was too heavy to carry the pain.

I told her, "Some of the kids are calling you names. They think you are a witch, Momma. And they call you an old maid."

Momma whispered, "I-I am really sorry that you have to go through that. You have seen God's glory and His amazing grace for yourself. Why are you ashamed of that? Why do you doubt that? Never doubt God."

Momma pulled out her scrapbook. It was full of prayers. "Whatever you have or will go through, there are prayers in here for those situations. Momma called it her closet prayers. Momma said, "Now dry your eyes and let me read you some of the prayers." I wiped the tears from my eyes as she read:

> Luke 24:17–18, 38
> And He said to them, "What kind of conversation is this that you have with one another as you

walk and are sad?" Then the one whose name was Cle-o-pas answered and said to Him, "Are You the only stranger in Jerusalem, and have you not known the things which happened there in these days?' And He said to them, "Why are you troubled? And why do doubts arise in your hearts?"

Psalm 126
When the Lord brought back the captivity of Zion, we were like those who dream. Then our mouth was filled with laughter, and our tongue with singing, and then they said among the nations, "The Lord has done great things for them." The Lord has done great things for us, and we are glad, Bring back our captivity, O Lord, as the streams in the south. Those that sow in tears shall reap in joy. He who continually goes forth weeping, bearing seed for the sowing, shall doubtless come again with rejoicing, bringing his sheaves with him.

I did not really understand what that meant at the time but I knew I felt better after that prayer. The next day at school, all the kids that were picking on me got in trouble. I know I had never told anyone at school about what they did to me and they knew I had not said a word to anyone about it either. One of them said that it was a curse that the Witch put on them. At that moment, I knew that God heard the prayer that Momma and I prayed. There's so much power in prayer if people would just take a moment out of their lives to try it. That little book that Momma put together was excellent.

I could not wait to get home from school so that I could tell my Momma what had happened. I was really excited and happy that God heard that prayer. The bus seemed to have taken the long way home that day. Finally, the bus stopped and I was home. I leaped for joy off the steps and ran as fast as my long, skinny legs would take me. At last, I made it to the door and went inside. All I could see was a dimmed room and I slowly walked inside. As I glanced around the room, there were a few candles burning in the candleholders. Then I saw Momma was on her knees with Miss Brown and her daughter Anna. Anna's nose had been bleeding for two weeks. She had seen many doctors and no one could stop the bleeding. Momma was at Anna's side, holding her hand so I shut the door and sat down in the living room waiting for my turn to talk to her.

I recall the room being dark but I could see the red, white, blue and gold candles burning. The light from the candles was reflecting off the walls and the ceiling in the room. Momma stopped praying aloud. Her lips were moving but you could not hear the words coming out of her mouth. I could feel myself being raised up in the air. The room lit up with those same small beautiful lights all over it. All of the small bubble lights had soft bright colors in them. Then all of a sudden, I felt myself being slowly let down but I could still feel the tingling, warm rays going through my body. I loved this feeling. I knew at the time that this is something bigger than I am. If I could live like this forever, I would be the happiest person on Earth.

The lights slowly moved out of the room and Anna jumped up off her knees shouting, "Mommy! My nose is not bleeding anymore! Thank you Ms. Juanita!"

Momma said, "No, don't ever thank me. You thank the Lord for hearing our prayers. God you are good. Lord, we want to thank you for your amazing healing powers."

Miss Brown was still sitting on the couch in shock. All she could do was hold her little girl while saying, "Thank you God for hearing and answering our prayers." She finally stood up and said, "Wow! What an experience! God is real and He has amazing powers." She was still in the zone.

She got up her nerve and asked, "What kind of prayer did you pray for God to hear you like that? God must really love you."

Momma told her, "Everyone is equipped to do this. It's just I have faith in the Lord. I believe that He will do what He promises."

Ms. Brown asked, "What prayer were you saying to yourself?"

Then Momma said, "I just reminded Him about the story that was in his book." Then Momma read the story to her:

> Luke 8:43–50
>
> Now a woman, having a flow of blood for twelve years, had spent all her livelihood on physicians and could not be healed by any. She came from behind and touched the border of His garment. And immediately her flow of blood stopped. And Jesus said, "Who touched me?" when all denied it. Peter and those with him said, "Master, the multitudes throng and press you, and you say, 'Who touched me'" But Jesus said, "Somebody touched me, for I perceived power going out of from me." Now when the woman saw that she was not hidden, she came trembling and, falling down before Him, she declared to Him in the presence of all the people the reason she had touched Him and how she was healed immediately. And He said to her, "Daughter, be of good cheer; your faith has made you well. Go in peace." While He was still speaking, someone came from the ruler of the synagogue's house, saying to him, "Your daughter is dead. Do not trouble the Teacher." But Jesus heard it and answered him, saying, "Do not be afraid; only believe, and she will be made well."

What Goes On In Momma's Closet

Luke 9:1–5

Then He called His twelve disciples together and gave them power and authority over all demons to cure diseases. He sent them to preach to the sick. And He said to them, "Take nothing for the journey, neither staffs nor bag nor money; and do neither bread nor money; and do not have two tunics apiece. Whatever house you enter, stay there, and from there depart. And whoever will not receive you when you go out of that city, shake off the very dust from your feet as a testimony against them."

Momma told her, "God back then is the same God that is in control right now. See Mrs. Brown, I do not have any magic broomsticks. The only magic I have is that I believe that God had a Son name Jesus Christ. I believe with all of my heart that He died on that cross for us. I believe that He died on that cross for our sins, our health, our strength, our faith and for whatever it is that we need. Now today you have to witness what He can do and who He is. I need you to give your life to Him. Read your Bible so you can know who He is. Please don't forget to give Him the glory." Mrs. Brown and Anna went out of the door. She started singing and praising His name. I even heard that she got deep into church but I never saw Anna or Mrs. Brown again.

A few weeks later Momma and I were in the Piggy Wiggly Store buying a few things for the house when I heard someone saying, "Hello Ms. Juanita. Thank you for praying for me. He also spoke to me.

Momma asked, "Do I know you?" I was thinking to myself that I did not know Momma knew someone in a wheelchair.

"Ms. Juanita, I am Jimmy," he replied. "Mrs. Smith's son Jimmy."

From a distance a familiar woman's voice shouted out, "Jimmy, where are you?"

He responded, "Right here Momma!" She began fussing at him about running off in the store.

Then she looked up and exclaimed, "Ms. Juanita!" She quickly grabbed Momma and hugged her super tight. "Thank you Juanita. Thank you so much for all of your prayers."

2

LEAVING THE PROBLEM IN GOD'S HANDS

Ring! Ring!

"Momma get the phone!" I yelled.

"You get the phone!" Momma demanded.

"Mmm-Hmm, okay," I replied as I rolled my eyes and stormed out the living room. I went down that long hallway to answer the phone.

"HELLO!" I shouted into the phone. Before I knew it, Momma walked behind me and popped me on the back of my head. Then she grabbed the phone.

"Hello, how can I help you? Thank you. I am fine and you. Okay, I am not sure if I could take another job right now." She pauses, "It's not that. Of course, Mrs. Smith, I can use the extra money. No, it's because school just let out for the summer and I don't have anyone to keep Maria. What? Are you sure? Okay. I will call her. Wait a minute! Let me go find a pen!"

"Maria, go get that pen out my purse," Momma demanded. I went to the purse and looked in it and I did not see a pen.

"Momma it's not one in here," I said.

"Bring my purse, Maria!"

"Okay Momma. Never mind, I see one on your bed."

"Okay Maria, bring it to me!" I passed Momma the pen. She went on to say in the phone: "Okay I will call her right away. Goodbye, Mrs. Smith. You have a good day too." Momma dialed the number on that new yellow phone that hung on the wall.

"Hello Mrs. Burk, I am Juanita. Mrs. Smith asked me to call you because you needed someone to work for you. Yes. Okay. Now you know that I charge seven dollars an hour. Oh!! Okay! It is? Well, I do not have anyone to take care of my baby girl and I will have to bring her with me. She is five years old. Oh! Yes ma'am. She is a good child. Oh yes, she is used to playing by herself. No she is not the only child. I have a son too. No. He is ten years old. Yes ma'am. He is not a problem, plus he is never here. He is always gone from the house," Momma laughed. "Are you sure everything is okay?

Well then. Sounds like I got a new job. Okay, I will see you on Monday at 11:00 a.m. Okay, you too. Bye!"

"Wake up! Juanita wake up!" I heard Momma say.

"What? Why?" Momma replied.

"Don't you have a job to go to today?" Grandma asked.

Momma asked Grandmomma, "What day is it?"

"It's Monday the 17th of May 1971 and its 8:00 a.m. I have breakfast on the table waiting on you." Grandma replied.

"Okay I am getting up," said Momma. I jumped out of bed and ran toward the table in the dining room.

Grandma said, "Hold up!! Where are you going?"

"I am going to eat," I replied.

"No you are not. Go wash your face and wash your teeth," said Grandma.

"Okay Granny," I replied.

As I headed to the bathroom, I heard Momma laughing.

"What are you laughing at Momma?" I asked. She laughed louder.

Momma said, "At you, silly." Then she started to sing, "This is the way we wash our face, wash our face, early in the morning." Before I knew it I was singing that crazy song with her. We finished up and then we went to the dining room so we could eat. Momma went into the hallway to use the phone.

She called Uncle Hersey because he owned the only cab company in town. Uncle Hersey answered, "Red Bird

Cab Company, this is Hersey." Momma asked him to send someone to pick her up. Then they started fussing because she never paid any of the drivers that ever picked her up. I could hear Uncle Hersey through the phone.

"See Juanita, you ain't nothing but a free loader!" yelled Uncle Hersey.

Momma replied, "Well, take care of our Momma. Now send somebody over here to pick me up so I can go to work because I am running late."

"Someone is on the way to get you, dammit!" Uncle Hersey yelled. The call ended, but minutes later Momma picked the phone back up and called him again. Just as Uncle Hersey answered the phone, a cab pulled up and honked outside of the house.

Uncle Hersey said, "Red Bird Cab Company, this is Hersey."

"Never mind, you devil!" Momma exclaimed as she hung up the phone. Momma and I laughed the whole time as we ran out the door to get into the cab.

"Hello Juanita. How are you doing?" the driver asked.

Momma said, "I'm okay, Joe. I just need a new brother.

Joe said, "Candy Man loves you.

She replied sarcastically, "I can't tell." They both laughed.

He said, "Where are we going?"

She said, "307 Madison." He said, "You are one of the few coloreds I know that can go over there across the tracks." They laughed and before we knew it we were crossing the tracks and headed up the hill to Mrs. Burks' house.

Momma said, "How much do I owe you?"

He giggled, "Don't worry about it Juanita. I will get the money from your brother."

We all could not help but stare at how big the house was. I had never seen a two-story house so pretty before. It was freshly painted white with black window shutters and it had a matching black door and a black roof. It was a big beautiful house. It was the prettiest house on the block. Their yard had perfectly trimmed bushes, colorful flowers and rose vines through the yard posts.

Momma said, "Come on let's go knock on the door, Maria." There was a peculiar, sweet smell coming from the many rose bushes that had my nose tingling. I knew it was summer because it smelled so good. As we went up the steps, I had to stop and look at the beautiful yellow flowers that were on both sides of the walkway that ran all the way down that long path up to the door. This was the prettiest yard that I had ever seen.

I said to Momma, "This looks like a house for a Barbie doll."

"I know baby," said Momma as Joe called her back to the cab.

"Ms. Juanita, I have a bad feeling in my gut."

"Why is that Joe?" asked Momma.

"Go ask that woman what time you get off work."

Momma said, "What for, Joe?"

He replied, "You know you should not be alone in this neighborhood, especially late in the evening."

"Stop acting crazy!" yelled Momma.

"Okay, Ms. Juanita, if you don't care about yourself that's fine but you have Maria with you. Do you want those white men to be after her?"

Momma replied, "No, of course not Joe. Okay hold up and let me see what time I will get off work." Momma walked to the door of the house and knocked on the door. I waited next to the taxi door.

"What do you want to be when you're all grown up, Maria?" asked Joe.

"I am not sure, yet." I replied. He laughs a little at the thought of me not knowing. Momma walked back to the taxi and said, "I'll be here only about three hours, Joe. Now are you happy?"

"Yes, Ms. Juanita I am. Call the Red Bird when you get off and tell Candy Man that I said I will come and pick you up."

Momma said, "All right Joe, I got to get to work. I will talk later. Bye for now."

"I'll be on my way then, Ms. Juanita. Bye Maria."

"Bye, Joe," I replied.

WHAT GOES ON IN MOMMA'S CLOSET

Work was somewhat hard on Momma because there was so much to do. Mrs. Burks was a nice woman, well for the brief moment I saw her. She had to leave as soon as we got there to carry on her errands. The time was over sooner than I thought it would be. Momma went to go use the phone in the kitchen.

"Redbird Taxi Stand, this is Joe."

"Hello Joe, it's me, Juanita. I am ready."

"Okay, Juanita, I am on my way over there."

"All right Joe, I will see you soon."

She hung up the phone and then called Mrs. Burks. "Well I finished everything for today. I just called for a taxi. Yes, ma'am he will be here in fifteen minutes."

Ms. Burks replied, "Okay Juanita, I am on my way over there." Momma and I sat on Mrs. Burks' blue antique couch. I could see out the window straight in the front yard.

"Momma I love this!" I exclaimed.

Momma asked me, "What is it that you love?"

I replied, "I love this house!"

Momma asked, "What is wrong with the house we have? Ours is brand new."

"Our house is okay, but this house is bigger than ours. I feel rich here."

Momma never replied. She just shrugged it off, but I think that rather sat with her a little. By the time we sat down good and got comfortable, Mrs. Burks pulled up outside and came in through the front door.

"You did a good job. It looks nice in here, and it smells fresh. They were right about you. You really are a hard worker. Thanks, Ms. Juanita. Here's your money." Momma reached her hand out and then she counted the money. "WAIT A MINUTE, MRS. BURKS! This amount is not right!"

"Mrs. Burks said, "All your money is there, Ms. Juanita. Take the money and leave."

"I cannot accept this much money from you like that."

Mrs. Burks said, "Why can't you?"

Momma said, "Mrs. Burks, I only worked for three hours and you have given me $27.00. You only owe me $21.00."

Mrs. Burks replied, "Don't you worry! Just go buy that pretty little girl something." "Thank you, Mrs. Burks. I will see you next Monday."

[Honk-Honk]

"Okay, Mrs. Burks! That's my ride. See you Monday."

"Juanita, you look tired," Joe exclaimed.

"I am tired. Mrs. Burks needed a lot of work done to her house in the little time I was there."

"Pretty hard work, huh?' "Yeah, but it was all worth it. Here's five dollars. I want you to take me to the store." We arrived at the store minutes later.

"Do you need me to wait for you?" Joe asked.

"No you can go ahead. We should be fine."

"Okay Juanita, I have another fare to go to, and it will tie me up. So are you sure?"

"Have a good day Joe!" Joe took that as a no, so he drove off as we headed into the store. The first thing that caught my eye were the big red, shiny apples.

I tugged at Momma's pants and exclaimed," Look Momma! Let's get some for Granny so we can bake an apple pie." I could imagine tasting the cinnamon-flavored apples and that buttery crust. I wanted everything that I saw. Everything looked good. I picked up a coke and asked Momma what it was. She told me it was a soft drink. So, I asked her if I could taste it. Then she put the drink in the buggy. We turned in the next aisle and my eyes lit up. All I could see were my favorite chips, Lays potato chips. I grabbed the bag and threw it into the buggy as well.

"Don't pick up anything else because we have to tote all the bags home."

"But Momma…"

"…But nothing. We have two miles to walk and carrying too much junk will wear your butt out."

All of a sudden, a voice came out of nowhere.

"Hello, Ms. Juanita," the voice said. I looked up, and it was a woman. She was super pretty with long silky black hair. Her skin was a caramel, reddish color. She had big, beautiful, brown eyes. She had the deepest dimples I had ever seen. She was just unbelievably beautiful.

Momma quickly introduced me to her, "Maria this is your Aunt Mimi."

"Huh?" I thought to myself.

She said, "This is your daddy's sister." "That's not even possible because Grandma said I don't have a daddy." Aunt Mimi laughed loud, and she was smiling so big that her dimples sank deep into her face. All I could do was stare at her the whole time. I had never seen a person that was that beautiful.

Momma said, "Say something to her."

I couldn't. I wanted to but the words were just stuck in my throat.

She told Momma, "That's okay! She does not know me. Juanita, I am very sorry for John's actions. I know what happened. She looks just like us. Maria, do you want to meet your daddy?"

I said, "Yes I do."

"Okay, I will make him come see you then."

We walked down the hill to the end of the parking lot and crossed the street. Momma said, "Wait a minute! The bags are too heavy. I need to rest." I was happy, because my bags were heavy too. We set the bags down on the sidewalk and then we sat down too. Both us were breathing hard.

Momma said, "It's going to rain. We need to keep going."

Bump! Bam! "George, come back here with my doll! I am going to whip you good!"

What Goes On In Momma's Closet

Momma and I looked up to see where all the commotion was coming from. I saw a little girl with real long flowing hair. She was about my height. Her skin looked pale and clear. She had green eyes. She was a pretty, skinny little girl. She said, "Hey! Why are you all sitting down there on my sidewalk?"

Momma said, "I am sorry but the bags were heavy. I am tired. Do you mind if we sit here for a minute–just long enough to catch our breath."

"I guess. As long as you are sitting there, can I play with your little girl?"

Momma said, "Okay, but not for long, because, it's going to rain."

"Okay, what is your name little girl?"

Momma said, "Her name is Maria."

"Come on Maria. Let's play." There was another loud sneeze as the front door opened again.

"Betsy, what are you doing? Who is that you are talking to?"

"Ma'am I am sorry!"

Betsy replied, "Momma this is my new best friend. Her name is Maria, and we are going to play so go back in the house." The thick woman came close and extended her hand to Momma and said, "I am sorry. My name is Ann. That's my big mouth daughter. She is a little lonely. Can Maria play with Betsy and her little brother George for a little while?"

. 41 .

Momma told her it was okay. "I am Juanita. Is there a phone I can use? I need to call a cab."

"Sure Ms. Juanita! Come on in." Betsy and I took off, running behind her house to play in her garage. I couldn't wait to swing around the six metal poles holding up the tin shed that protected us from the sun beaming through the rain clouds. I swung around the first pole and then she followed me. We took turns singing and laughing uncontrollably about nothing.

Joe pulled up in his cab and hung his head out the window. "Come on Maria. Let's go."

Betsy said, "Don't take her away from me. She's my best friend." Joe told her that he was sorry. "I will bring her back one day to play with you." Betsy called him a liar and ran in the house crying.

Momma said goodbye to Ms. Ann and little George. Joe drove off.

"Juanita, I don't think that is a good idea to let Maria play over there because Ms. Ann's husband is a bad man. They are always arresting him for something. He can't hold his alcohol down well. He gets real abusive to his wife and kids." Joe said.

Uncle Hersey called Joe on the cab CB radio and asked if he had picked up Juanita.

Joe responded, "Yes, I picked up that package."

"Well when you drop her off, go get your wife. She just called and said she was ready."

"10-4 and out, Candy."

Uncle said, "10-4 and out."

Five minutes later we were at home. Momma gave Joe two more dollars. Then he helped take the groceries into the house.

"All right I will see you later," said Joe. Everyone said goodbye and Joe drove off. We put the groceries up. I grabbed the bag of apples and took it to Granny.

"Look Granny! Look at what I have for you," I exclaimed.

She laughed, "I guess you want an apple pie."

I told her, "I sure do. Will you make it for me?"

"Yes, I will bake it tomorrow." I was happy. I hugged Granny very tight.

"Maria, your water is ready," said Momma.

"Okay, Momma, I'm coming," I said.

Momma walked me into the bedroom. We got on our knees and said, "Now I lay me down to sleep. I pray to the Lord my soul to keep. He lives in me while sleep or wake, and He blesses me for goodness' sake. If I should die before I wake. I pray to the Lord my soul to keep. Amen."

I still could not sleep. Normally that prayer gave me so much comfort but this night was different. All night long, I tossed and turned. Momma was standing over me.

"Get up sleepy head. Go wash your face and eat breakfast."

"Okay Momma." I jumped up with Betsy on my mind. She was getting ready to go to work. Granny told her that she did not feel that good.

Momma asked her, "Do you want to go to the doctor?" Granny told her no. "Do you want me to take Maria with me today?"

"No, she will be fine here."

Momma gave me a new set of clothes to put on. "Wow! When did I get this Momma? It's so pretty. Momma you know that I love bright colors. This pink overall is going to be my favorite outfit."

"Maria, do not get dirty. Your daddy is coming in town today."

"Okay. What did you say Momma? My daddy is coming to see me?"

"Yes. Stay in the house and watch television with your Granny."

"Okay."

Momma was walking out the door. Granny hollers out to her not to fill my head up with that daddy nonsense.

"Bye! I love you."

"I love you too."

"I will be good today."

The door shut. I helped Granny with breakfast and cleaned the dishes. Then we went into the living room and watched television.

Granny said, "It's twelve o'clock. Now you have to be quiet. My show is coming on. Go outside and play." I walked outside, and then I peeked back into the house to see if Granny was deep into watching her show. She was. Then I tiptoed down our long driveway. I looked both ways and then I crossed the street. I ran as fast as I could go down the street. I ran seven blocks. My heart was beating so fast. I knew that I had to rest for a minute. I could barely catch my breath. I stopped to bend over and put my hands on my knees. I caught my breath and started back walking again. I had to see my first best friend again. Finally, I was by Betsy's house. One more block to go. I could see Betsy and little George playing in the front yard. I stopped, and the fear took over my mind. I couldn't make the voices in my head stop. What if she doesn't want to play with me? What do I say to her? I started to turn around.

Then I heard, "Maria! Maria! You came back!" Betsy started running to me and I ran to her. We hugged each other. I was so happy. I had a friend that really wanted to be my friend. She didn't know about the names the other kids called me. I had a real friend. We played and played. Her mom called her into the house.

Betsy said, "Wait a minute Mom!" Betsy told me to wait a minute. I stood outside the house and waited. A few seconds later, she was back outside with a needle in her hands.

Betsy said, "You are going to be my blood sister. I never want to lose you. I love you. Now, I need to stick you with this needle. Then I will stick myself. Then we need to rub our blood together so that we can be blood sisters."

I said, "That looks like it will hurt."

She said, "Stop being a baby. I love you. You said that you love me. Now give me your finger."

"Ouch! That hurts." She laughed at me. Then she stuck herself. We rubbed our fingers together.

She said, "Now we are blood sisters. How does it feel?"

"Good! I feel good."

Betsy said, "I prayed for a sister."

"I did too."

"Betsy! Get in this house and eat."

"No Momma, only if my blood sister can come in and eat too!"

"Okay just come in and eat."

We walked through that loud, squeaky door.

Her mother, Ann said, "Y'all, wash your hands and come sit down."

Betsy splashed me with water in my face from the sink. I splashed her back with water. We laughed. I grabbed her hand and we walked and sat down at the table. Ms. Ann was singing and fixing our plates.

Betsy said, "She can't cook." We laughed. The chicken was nasty, but the macaroni was really good. The macaroni was so cheesy. They were so good. Squeak! The squeaking door opened again. Bam! I told her that door is loud.

She said, "I know!"

We heard, "I be dognap! Did I hear a jig-a-boo in my freaking house! Ann please tell me I didn't hear that."

Ann said, "Baby, what are you doing home so early?"

"Don't you get off subject!"

Betsy said, "OOOhhh MY!" Before she could finish, we heard footsteps getting closer and closer. My gut tells me this is not going to be good. I am shaking with fear of not knowing what's about to happen! I started praying in my head, God is my refuge and my strength. Lord help me! I didn't know why I was praying but my gut told me this was a good time to pray.

The short, pale man bent down to the table and said, "Who told you that you could bring your black self in here and eat my freaking food up? That food I work my tail off to get."

I was so scared that I couldn't speak. I couldn't say one word. He stood back up and turned around and walked back though the living up toward the front door. He turned left into the bedroom.

"Ann, I can't freaking believe you got a dam chick-a-boo sitting in my freaking living room, eating the food I freaking worked hard to get. Slap! Slap!

We jumped from the loud slap sound. Betsy's eyes were as big as a fifty-cent piece, and I know mine were too. Betsy said to hide in the closet. I did. I was shaking so hard in the closet that the broom was vibrating on the side of me. I could hear all of them hollering and crying. It was too tense in here. I was so confused. I didn't understand what a chick-a-boo or a jig-a-boo was. Whatever it meant, I know that is what I was. I heard the hard, strong footsteps coming back toward the dining room. I put my hand over my mouth to keep from screaming.

Her daddy looked around the room and said, "Where did the little colored girl go? Are you hiding her?"

I could see through the air vents that were in the closet doors. Betsy shook her head no. Her eyes were still very big, and her heart you could see it beating hard from the closet.

He said, "Betsy you are lying to me because of a nigger. I can't believe you would take up for a freaking black girl. Are you choosing a colored over your daddy?"

"No, daddy. While you were slamming the mess out of Momma, she got scared and ran out the door."

Little George said, "That black girl ran down the street." I was real scared then. The mop moved in the closet.

What Goes On In Momma's Closet

Her daddy said, "I will be damned! You lie to me and you got your brother lying too. I am going to beat your butts when I come back in from hanging her little black ass!"

I peeped through the vents of the closet door. He walked back to the bedroom. Then he went outside. Betsy came to the closet, opened the door, and said, "Why did you move? He is going to beat the hell out of me and little George! I am going to try to get you out of here okay?" I nodded.

She grabbed my hand and we ran out the house. Bam! The door slammed hard behind us. Bam! Then it bounced off the old chip, wood frame. Bam! We took off running. Little George said, "Daddy! The little nigger is getting away!"

Betsy was running and talking, "Please don't tell anyone what happened, okay?" I told her okay.

"Betsy! Betsy! Are you trying to find that little nigger? I am going to beat you! You better stop and come here. You better bring that nigger back with you."

Betsy said, "Run and don't stop for no one. You hear me? Keep running! I love you!" I kept running.

Five houses later, my brother's best friend's grandmother, Mary Bell, was taking out trash. She said, "Hey come here!" I froze in my steps. She walked up to me, grabbed my arm and said to come in the house. She pulled me up her long driveway. I was still stiff as a board. We were standing in the side door. Before I knew it, she was holding both of my arms. She was bending down to my level and the she looked me straight in the eyes.

"What are you running from? O my God you are trembling." I felt her shaking me. "I saw you playing at that house. I started to pick you up and take you when I had a ride. Did that man touch you?" I shook my head. Tears started flowing down my face. Roar! Her side door was open. The roaring sound got louder.

She said, "Run and hide under there and stay until I tell you to come out."

"Okay!" I shook my head and went to hide under the bed.

I heard three different voices yelling, "Niggers, come out here. Right now!" I watched Mary walk to her closet that was across from the bed I was hiding under. She stood up on her tiptoes and reached into a hatbox that was sitting on top of her closet. She pulled out a shiny, silver gun. She called on God to help her.

She said, "Lord, this is bigger than I am. Lord God I call on you so you can help me. Please help me, Lord, Jesus! It's too many of them to fight. I am going to leave this in your hands. Amen."

I grabbed my mouth to keep myself from screaming. She came down off her tiptoes. She stood in her door with the gun behind her back.

I heard, "Hey nigger! Have you seen a little, black girl?"

"No, I haven't. Why you want to know?"

"I am going to kill her. You tell her that."

Mary Bell said, "I am not telling her nothing now get out my damn yard!"

"Hey George, I bet she is hiding that little nigger in her house.

"Ain't I got her in here."

George said, "Let us check your house." I heard them jumping out of the truck. "We are coming in to search your house!"

Bell said, "The devil is a lie. If you come in here, you won't leave the way you came. I am going to send you to that damn master you serve! Plus the police is on their way."

"George, get back in the truck. I am not going to jail for no damn nigger."

"George, you must love being in jail. Now get in your damn trucks and get out my damn driveway."

I could hear the wheels peeling backward. My heart was racing. Ms. Mary Bell backed up out the door and put the gun up so I couldn't see it. She told me to get up and come here. I slowly got out from behind the bed. My body was still shaking.

She said, "Wait here! I need to call your uncle and tell him to come get you." I was still confused about what had happened. My first mind told me to wait there, but I kept hearing my best friend say, "Promise me, "You won't tell anyone." I heard the truck go back down the street toward

Betsy's house and it parked. I heard Mary Bell on the phone with Joe. I tiptoed to the side door. I took off up the street to the top of the hill. I heard the truck start up again. Oh my God! My brain was going crazy.

Then I remembered that prayer that Ms. Mary Bell was saying, "God please help me. I can't fight those grown men. It's one too many of them, I need you right now. Lord, I am going to put it your hands. Lord have your way and let your will be done. Amen!"

The truck sound got closer. I could hear Mary Bell calling my name. I ran to the big willow tree that was in the yard at the side of me. I hid behind the willow tree. As they were passing me by, I heard them talking about me.

"She could not be that far away!" I heard.

"Don't worry George. We will find her. Just keep looking in between the houses."

I peeped out from behind the tree, and I saw three men on the back of an old Ford truck dressed up in white sheets. I poked my head back behind the tree until they disappeared. I started running again after they were out of sight.

I heard, "Maria, Why are you running? Come here!" I kept running. The attorney's wife called me and again. I kept running. I heard her call her son Junior.

"Come here now, let's go and get in the car."

By that time, I was at full speed and down the hill. All I could see was an open field. I stopped and hid behind a big dumpster. I had to plan this very carefully. I jumped up and took off again. I heard the truck coming back down the street. It was too late. I was in the middle of the field by that time.

I heard someone say, "There she is." The driver was driving so fast he didn't hear them until he had turned.

George said, "I told you to slow down."

"Don't worry we will catch her at the next block." I heard the old Ford truck pick up speed.

My biggest fear had just come true. I knew I didn't have a chance in Hell of making it across that big open parking lot. It was open duck season and I was the duck. I knew I was going to be a sitting duck.

"Lord here I am again. Help me please!" I started running faster up another hill.

I heard "Maria, is that you?" I stopped, panting. I looked up and saw Pam.

Pam asked me, "What is wrong with you?" I told her there were some bad men after me.

She said, "Come in here and let me hide you." I walked in her house, and her brothers were in the living room. She had five brothers.

One of the brothers said, "Look at that colored girl. She looks like she saw a ghost." They laughed at me and walked outside. I heard roar! Roar! Zoom! The truck zoomed past the house. I was relieved. I heard wheels peeling backward.

It finally stopped right in front of the house. I peeped out the window and I saw that old Ford truck in front of the house. Smoke was coming out the tailpipe. I saw one of the men that were sitting in the back of the old Ford playing with some rope in his hand.

He said, "Hey partner have you all seen a little nigger?" They said nope.

George said, "We just saw her run up this hill.

The little brother said, "Are you calling us a liar? "

George said, "Well no! I don't understand how that little nigger could have just disappeared."

They jumped off the truck and walked though the yard. Then they got back on that truck. I heard one of Pam's brothers say, "What are you going to do to her?

"Lynch her!"

The brother said, "I might have seen her. Do you have some money?"

George said, "No!"

The brother said, "You ain't got no money! What did she do to you to make you want to hang her?

George said, "Her black behind was sitting at my table eating my food."

Pam's biggest brother said, "What? Is that it? Then you need to lynch your wife."

George said, "Have you seen her or not?"

"Yeah we saw her." They laughed.

My heart stopped as I peeped out the window.

George said, "Who is that peeking out your window?"

There was silence. Everyone turned toward the window and looked. I couldn't move. My feet were stuck. I froze in mid-air. Bam! My face was on the floor. I tried to wiggle my feet but nothing moved. Finally, I was able to get my head up. I saw Pam standing in the window, waving good-bye to them.

They said at the same time, "Want to take my sister instead?" Then all of them laughed.

The little brother said, "Yes, I saw her. She went that way. I told you I saw her running down the streets that way."

The big brother came in the house and said to me, "Look, I don't know which way you need to go but we told him that you went that way. Take off and go! Hurry up!"

I took off as fast as I could. Finally I made it home. I flew inside the house.

Granny said, "What was that?" She was on the phone. "Hold on! Something just flew past me."

By the time she had put the phone down I was back under the bed. I was scared to death. All I wanted to do was stay under that bed until I died. My mind was traveling too fast for me.

"Hey, who is that in here? I peeped out from under the bed. I still couldn't talk. I saw her feet get closer to me. I closed my eyes tight. I heard a loud. Click! I knew Granny had her gun. I started breathing harder. She was standing right over my head with her gun cocked. I knew without a doubt it was my time to die. She took some steps backwards and pointed that cocked gun toward the bed. I could see her looking down. She slowly bent down. I just closed my eyes. I couldn't believe it. I just barely got away from my best friend's daddy's house with my life. Just to come home and die.

As Granny bent down to her knees, she said, "Come out little Devil. I want to see who I am going to put a bullet in. Come out! Come out! Don't be scared now! Come out so I can put a hole in you!"

I tried hard to say something but my words were just stuck in my throat. Next, she pulled the bedspread up that hid me. I saw the gun barrel in my face.

I heard Momma say, "Are you okay?"

Granny replied, "I am okay it was just Maria. You sure did get over here fast. We were just on the phone."

Uncle Hersey walked up to me and said, "What's wrong with you? Are you okay? Tell me what happened." I still was unable to talk.

Uncle Hersey said, "I know you hear me talking to you. I can't help you if you don't tell me."

I shook my head and said nothing was wrong with me. I kept hearing Betsy say, "Don't tell a soul about what happened, okay?"

"Nothing happened Uncle Hersey."

He got mad and said, "She is going to be crazy just like her mother." He looked at me and said, "Why are you lying? My phone was ringing off the hook. Everybody in town is looking for you. They are going to hurt that man. Tell me what happened!"

I was so scared so I told him nothing happened. He got mad and stormed out the door and said, "Fine! Have it your way!" Then he got in his car and drove off. I wanted to tell him but I didn't know how. I wanted say thank you. I love you for caring about me but instead I just balled up all of the pain inside me and held on to them. The tears just started rolling down my face as I watched Uncle Hersey's cab drive off. I just stood there and watched him leave. The pain in my heart grew heavier and my tears got bigger.

Part Two of My Book
―――――

"This is a good prayer to accept the Lord into your life." Auntie made me read the bible in front of all those people. I was scared to read it, however I knew my heart was still broken because I had lost the friend/blood sister that I had prayed to God for. All I knew was that I wanted her back, so I made the sacrifice. I prayed.

Finally, I was finished reading that passage. Then she looked me in the eye and said, "It's not the most comfortable sensation in the world, but tension is not always a bad thing, in fact, it can often bring out the best in you. A stressful situation can give your creativity and intelligence a satisfying jolt. So stop seeking out people who are completely compatible with you. If you surround yourself with only like-minded thinkers, your own mind and soul will no longer be challenged, and they will no longer grow."

I did not understand what that meant. People were saying, "Amen." The spirit was still moving around in that restaurant. We picked up the trash that was on the table and threw away the trash into the trashcan. Then, we headed to the exit door. I stood by the door while she went back to the table. She grabbed her bible and put it back in her purse. We headed out the door, and got in her beautiful, white 1967 Pontiac. She started up the car, looked at her watch, and said, "Its 7:30 pm. No wonder it looked like it was getting dark out here." The moth stand was right around the corner from my house. Auntie made a right turn at the red light and four houses down was my driveway. We pulled into the driveway and she drove up to the carport. She turned off the car and said, "I know that I told you a lot of things today, but one thing that I want you to remember is, never give up on God because when everyone else turns their back on you, He will be there. Do you understand what I just said to you?" I said, "Yes TT, I do. What you are saying is to never lose your faith in God, right Auntie?" She reached over, grabbed me, and said, "Sister Girl, you are going to be okay." We smiled and walked into the house.

Momma gave me a hug and kissed me. She asked me was I okay? I told her yes and she told me to go take a bath. I went to the bathroom and took off my clothes. The bath water was already prepared for me. I put both of my feet in the water and slipped deep in the warm waters. I laid my back up against the back of the tub's wall, and I just relaxed. I heard, "Wake up before you drown in that tub." I was still full from all of the food that I had eaten. Momma bathed me and pulled me out the tub, and then she checked my body for any bruises. She helped me put on my clothes and then we walked to the bedroom. We got on our knees to say our prayers. She kissed my head, tucked me into the bed, and walked out of the room.

The next morning, Granny was sicker. Momma told me to get dressed, so we could go to the doctor. Momma called Uncle Hershey to come pick us up. She asked Granny to get out of the bed so she could get dressed, but Granny told Momma she could not get up. Momma went to the closet and found her a pink soft dress to put on. Momma gave Granny a bath, then I heard Uncle Hershey come through the door and walk down the hallway. Momma said, "We are back here in Momma's room." He walked in the door of the bedroom and then he stepped right back out. He said, "Y'all call me when you all are through with the clothes thing." I laughed at him. He was looking serious like he always does. Momma and Granny were laughing at him under their breaths. Momma finished putting Granny's clothes on her, then she called Uncle Hershey back in the room so he could help get her in the car. I walked outside with them. I noticed Uncle Hershey had a new red, Buick car. It was beautiful. I said to Uncle Hershey, "I like your new Buick." He said, "Thanks." He had a big, beautiful smile on his face. I said, "Uncle, you must love the color red?" He replied, "Yes I do."

They finally got Granny into the car. Granny began grunting from the pains that she felt in her chest. Uncle Hershey said, "We will be at the hospital in no time, Momma." He had mounted a CB radio in his personal car so he could keep up with his business. We heard someone call his radio. They wanted him to pick up one of his regulars. He told them that he was not going to be able to do it because he was taking his mother to the hospital. Granny told him to go ahead and make some money, because she would be with some doctors that would take care of her. She also told him that if things got worse Juanita would call him. Momma said, "Uh Uh!" Uncle Hershey told Granny, "Okay."

Uncle Hershey pulled up to the emergency room door. He got out of the car and went inside the hospital. He came out of the hospital with a wheelchair and put Granny in it. He then pushed her into the hospital. He walked to the back of the hospital and came back with a full staff. They got Granny and placed her in a room. I had to sit in the waiting room while they worked on Granny. While I was waiting, I heard a man that was sitting behind me say, "I know they just didn't take that nigger to the back!" He stood up, upset, and walked to the front part of the emergency room demanding an answer to as why they took my Granny before him. The nice nurse told him that it was because she was having chest pain and heart problems, and they come before a bad stomach cramp. He said, "But that's a nigger! She comes after me!" He then stormed out of the hospital.

Several hours passed by before we heard anything, but finally, a thick, colored nurse came out, and walked towards me. She said, "Hello Maria. I am Hershey's wife. Do you remember me?" I shook my head. She said, "It's okay, it has been a long time since I've seen you all. Where are your Momma and Herman?" I told her that Herman was spending the summer with his friend James, and Momma went to get something for me to eat. "When your mother gets back, tell her that, Dorothy, Hershey's wife was looking for her." I said okay. She walked around the corner and disappeared. Momma came back from another corner with some milk and a bowl of cornflakes. She passed it to me. I told her that Aunt Dorothy came looking for her. Momma ran around the corner and disappeared. I jumped when I heard Momma howl from around the corner. I knew it was not going to be good news, so I walked to the corner and peeked. I saw Aunt Dorothy holding Momma and saying, "Juanita, you are going have to pull it together. Yes, they called code blue on her, and Her heart keeps stopping. You have Maria in the waiting room. Now I have called Mary-Helen and Hershey and told them already. Hershey is on his way back here. Now, you all do not need to be fighting up here okay. Mary-Helen said her and the girls will head out first thing in the morning. I do not have room for them over at my house, but their daddy Willie Gray does. Now look at me Juanita, you just have to keep your faith. Go to the chapel and pray. I get off in a few hours and I will take Maria home with me." Momma nodded her head to say yes.

Momma flew past me, so I do not think she saw me standing there. I followed her as she turned and walked down a long hallway. She turned right and walked into the chapel. She bent down on her knees and started talking to God. Normally it takes a minute for me to see the brighten light that lit up the room but this time it did not take long at all. I believed God felt her pains. His Holy Spirits filled the room. I danced around in the tiny bright lights that were all over the room. I felt myself falling, and down I went. I realized that I had bounced around and tripped over momma legs. She looked up. I said to myself, "Oops, I just messed up." Momma looked at me with tears in her eyes and said, "Where did you come from?" She grabbed me and held me tight. I asked her if she was okay. She said, "I love you, ok." I asked, "Are you okay? Is Granny going to die?" At this point, I had tears in my eyes. I could not see myself living without Granny. Momma could not cook, and she was always busy taking care of other people. I knew she did not have time for me. Momma assured me that she was going to be fine. She said that God had given her a vision and he told her that. We walked back to the waiting area and sat down. Aunt Dorothy said goodbye to the second shift workers.

Aunt Dorothy walked to me and said, "Let's go get some ice cream." She did not have to tell me twice. I jumped up, took her hand, and said, "Let's go!" She said, "You want to spend the night at my house." I said, "Yes, Aunt Dorothy." I told Momma goodbye. I headed to the moth stand that was right down the street. The woman that was there yesterday took our order. We both ordered a hamburger, fries, and a coca-cola, then we ordered our ice cream. The food was very good and we both were full. Neither one of us wanted to get up from the table. We laughed at each other because we were so full. I fell in love with my Aunt Dorothy, because she was one of the sweetest women I had ever met.

We cleaned up our mess and headed to her house. She pulled up in her front yard and said, "That school that is across the street is the school that you will be attending in two weeks." I said, "That means after school I can stop by your house." She said, "That's perfect because I get off from work before you get home." We both smiled. She opened her car door, and we got out of the car. I walked in the door behind her. She put some food on the stove for Uncle Hershey. I asked her what was she was cooking. She said meatloaf, because she could stick it in the oven while we took a nap. I said, "I'm not sleepy, can I go out and play instead?" She said, "Yes." I saw her go lay down.

I remembered that my blood sister stayed about ten blocks from Aunt Dorothy's house. I thought to myself, "I need to go check on my best friend." I walked out of Auntie's house and sat down on the warmed concrete on her front porch. I stared at the school that I would be starting in two weeks, and then I looked up at the beautiful sky. The skies looked clear, while the sun's rays bared down hard. It was a nice, hot summer day. I soon got tired of sitting down on the hot concrete because the thoughts were back in my head, "Go checkout your blood sister." I decided I was going to go, and I walked off the porch and eased down the street.

3

MAKING TIME FOR GOD

I COULD NOT believe that I had talked myself into leaving. I walked up the streets to go to Betsy's house. I remembered being on top of the hills, looking down the streets, and seeing Betsy and Little George on the front porch. I walked faster to get to, while she looked up and saw me. She started smiling and walked toward me and they met me halfway up the street. We held hands and walked back to her porch. I asked Betsy, "Why does your daddy not like me? What did I do to him?" George walked out the house and said, "It's because you are a nigger." He looked so serious when he said it. I did not understand that. I asked, "What is a nigger?" Betsy said, "People with your color of skin" I said, "Wow! Seriously, he does not like me because of the color of my skin?" Betsy said, "He is just crazy." Before she could finish explaining it to me, Mrs. Ann walked out to the front porch and joined us. I looked at her face and was confused. Her face had bruises all over it, and her body had belt marks all over her. All her bruises just put me in a state of shock. How could someone love you and put all of those bruises on your body? I hated what had happen to them, but I was very thankful that he did not catch me. I said to myself, "Thank you Lord for hearing my cries of fear."

I felt my body being shook, then I heard Maria say, "Get up, I need to show you something." Betsy was pulling my body away from the porch. She took me to the side of the house and said, "LOOK AT ME!" She rose up her dress and said, "I have been beaten to. He said when he finds you he is going to kill you." My body went back into shock mode again. I felt my body being pulled again. This time she was taking me towards the open shed that we use to play under. I looked at it good. I said, "That looks like a big play house now." I was thinking that we could play under it and the sun would not burn our bodies. The fears started easing up and I felt more relaxed. I guess I said it aloud because she said, that playhouse is not going to be my death house. She took me inside and showed me an old, white five-gallon paint bucket. Betsy said, "Daddy was going to make you stand on the top of this bucket." Then Little George said, "He was going to put your neck in here. Betsy and George said HUMM Hum!! Then, he was going to kick the bucket out from under your feet and your body would have flown up to the roof." Betsy said, "Your body would have dangled and shook as if you were a little rag doll. You would have stayed there until you died." I did not like what I had heard, so I looked all around the garage. I looked around the shed. I looked at all of the junk that was in there. He could have hid my body under anything out there and no one would have known. Betsy shook me, and I realized that I was in a daze. She said, "Stop crying. It will be okay. You will always be my sister. That man that was hanging was the same man that was getting ready to take you in the brushes." "What? He was the man that lost his kitty cat in the woods?," I asked. "Yep" Do you think that he was going to hurt us?" My tears started drying up. "Oh! Yes, Maria. That weird scar face man was going try to touch our booties. Maria you can't come back over here anymore, okay? I will find you when I get grown." Before she could finish her sentence, I was half way down the street.

Aunt Dorothy opened up the screen door and asked me if I was hungry. I did not respond. She looked down at me and asked me if I was okay. I did not say anything. She said, "Your Momma is on her way to get you, but you need to eat. Come in this house you look like you are about to have a heat stroke." I went to the bathroom and washed my hands, and then I came back to the table and sat down in front of the meatloaf that Aunt Dorothy had fixed. I had no intentions on eating. The meatloaf's aroma went up my nose. The mashed potatoes were loaded with all of my favorite ingredients inside of them. It had cheese, chopped ham, bacon, chives and to top it all off, sour cream. The sweet peas even looked good. She made the best yeast rolls. I could not hold back any longer, so I dove into my plate. That is how I decided that Aunt Dorothy earned the title of being the best cook in the family.

I heard someone say, "Knock-Knock." I turned around and saw Momma. She said, "What is that that I smell? It smells so good." Before she could finish the statement, Aunt Dorothy had a plate in her hands. She sat the plate down on the table and said, "I knew you were hungry. You are always starving. If you learned how to cook you wouldn't be so hungry." They both laughed. Then she asked, "How is Momma Eleanor doing?" Momma said, "She is stable now, but she is sleeping."

Momma offered to wash dishes, but Aunt Dorothy would not let her. She grabbed her keys and took us to the house. We went into the house and Momma said, "You smell like the great outdoors. It is bath time for you." I remember getting into the nice, warm water and just relaxing.

I woke up the next morning to hearing someone knocking on the door. I shouted to Momma and told her someone was knocking on the door, so we walked to the door together. Momma opened up the door and I saw this little girl standing in front of me. It was as if I was looking in a mirror. She appeared out of nowhere. I wanted to know where she had come from because I was so confused. How could I have a twin? I did not have a sister, but this girl resembled me. We had the same hair and eye color. We were also the same height and size. All I could do was stare at her. I was so amazed looking at my twin. Then I heard a loud horse voice and it broke my stare. Momma said, "Tell your daddy, hello." I looked up very slow because the deep voice was still ringing in my ear. I saw a tall, muscular man standing in front of me that reminded me of what Bigfoot would look like. He said, "HELLO!" I jumped behind Momma, so she could do her motherly duties and protect me from that Bigfoot. I felt a tug on my nightclothes. My twin had a voice of an angel. She said, "Come play with me. Come on you are my sister." I held on to Momma legs tighter. She turned to Bigfoot and said, "She won't play with me daddy! Why won't my sister play with me? Make her play with me right now!" The man bent down and said, "I am John. I am your daddy, and you need to play with your sister." My eyes got big as a fifty-cent piece. I released Momma's leg, and I took off down the hallway. I shot under the bed and pulled the cover down halfway to the floor so they could not see me. I heard that little girl, which looked like me, tell her daddy to find me. The phone rang, and then I heard nine different footsteps coming toward me.

Momma said, "Look under the bed and you will find her." I could feel my heart beating at a rapid pace. I was so scared. Then, I remembered the last time that I was under the bed. I was under the bed hiding from Betsy's daddy. My heart began beating at a faster pace. "Thump! Thump! Pop!" I saw a set of eyes looking at me. "Daddy, here she is. Get her out from under this bed." I felt a strong pull and I was sitting on top of the bed. The little girl said, "My name is Lisa. I am your sister. Do you not like me?" I nodded my head to tell her that I did like her. She said, "Well let's play together." I heard, "Don't make that little punk play with you! Let's go." The next thing I knew I was up in the air and then falling down to the bed. I bounced off the bed and ran back under the bed. Lisa said, "Daddy! Why did you do that? She was going to play with me?" He told her, "Come on, let's go. I had enough of this."

Momma was on the phone. Daddy stormed past her. He was mad. Momma called his name. Lisa was crying. "No Daddy, I don't' want to go. I want to play with my sister." He said, "Well stay here. I am leaving." Momma dropped the phone and then ran outside behind him. I heard her say, "Where are you going? I didn't make this baby by myself. You remember that, you drunk bastard! You took me." I heard this ear-piercing, sound backing up out the driveway. He stuck his head out the window and said, "Your crazy little girl won't come from under the bed. What do you

What Goes On In Momma's Closet

want me to do?" He stuck his head back in the car and drove off. Momma ran back to the phone and said to the person on the line, "I'm sorry for leaving you on hold." I sat down in the living room and stared out of the window. I thought about the prayer I had prayed to God. I thanked God that I had a big sister. I thought about what I will do the next time I saw her. I could go outside and play with her. Then, I thought about what Momma said about him taking her and it was not her fault that she had me. At this point, my little mind just shut down. I went outside under our carport and played with my Barbie doll and Barbie doll pool. I told my Barbie Betsy, "It's not my fault that you was born." I named her Betsy after my best friend. I walked in the house and Momma was still on the telephone. I looked in the kitchen drawer and got some scissors. I heard Momma giving somebody some directions to our house. I put the scissors behind my back and walked outside. I picked up Betsy. I told Betsy that she was a bad best friend and I cut her hair off. I heard Momma say, "I will see you in a minute." She hung up the phone and walked towards me. Momma walked to the side door with a big smile on her face. She opened up the door and said, "It has been twenty minutes." I look down at all the hair and I tried to slide right on top of it but it was too late. I saw her eyes gaze down at the hair that was everywhere. She froze in her traces and said, "Where is your doll's hair? Why did you cut her hair off?" I just paused. She went in the house and came back with a belt. I took off to the backyard, but I knew she could catch me. I ran into the woods and came out at the carwash. I hooked a left turn and ran past three houses, and I made it back to the house while she was still in the woods looking for me. I ran up the long driveway and slid back under the bed. I could hear the kids across the streets saying she is in the house. The front door opened. Momma stepped back outside. A car was pulling into the driveway. I heard Momma say, "O My Sweet Jesus!" A proper voice said, "Juanita I haven't seen you since 1972, and now it's 1975. It has been almost four years since I seen you. You haven't changed a bit, not one bit." I thought to myself, "I'm almost nine years old and I don't remember that voice at all."

A little girl voice said, "Aunt Juanita, hello. Why do you have a belt in your hand?" Momma said, "It was for Maria." I heard some little girls laugh. I climbed out from behind the bed and walked to the front door. I peeked out the door and saw a woman that looked like Momma. The woman looked at the door and saw me. She said, "Come here Maria. Come give me a hug and meet your family." I walked outside and gave her a big hug. She said, "This is Tamera, Angela, Karen, and my baby girl, Mary Joe." She had a big bucket of K.F.C. She gave the chicken to Momma and told us to go in the house so we could eat.

Then she said, "Juanita, I'm going to the hospital to check on Momma." She drove off. We went in the house to eat, and after we ate, Karen started playing on the phone. She got numbers from the telephone book and called random people's houses. She asked crazy things like "Is your washing machine running?" If the person on the other end of the phone said "yes," then she would tell them, "Well, you better go and catch it." We would burst out laughing. We all took turns doing it. Angela told me to call the operator and curse them out. I stuck my finger in the round hole on the receiver part of the phone. I rolled the dial to the number zero on the phone and put the phone to my ear. The woman on the other side of the phone said, "This is the operator. How can I help you?" I said, "Female dog, you can't help me! Kiss my butt!" I kept cursing her out. They were laughing, uncontrollably until they were crying. I was thinking, "Boy I could have my own comic show." I started laughing too. I was so amused until I started crying too. I had to hang up the phone.

Momma came around the corner and wanted to know why we were so loud. We still were laughing. We were so tickled until she started laughing too. Everyone was having a good time. Aunt Mary Helen walked in the front door and joined in on the laughter. She wanted to know what was so hilarious. Everyone glimpsed at each other, but no one said a word, we just laughed harder. Then the yellow phone, that hung on the wall, rang. We walked into the living room smiling at each other.

Aunt Mary told Momma that Momma Eleanor was coming home tomorrow around twelve in the afternoon. Momma said, "That is good. I'll have Hershey to pick her up." Aunt Mary said, "That's alright. I will pick her up. Hershey see's Momma all the time. I don't see her often." Momma replied, "Hershey needs to pick her up because he has to lift her and put her in the car." Then Aunt Mary said, "Juanita, you need to remember that I am a nurse I am use to lifting people up." The phone rang again. Aunt Mary said, "I got it." She answered the phone and said, "Hello?" We heard her say, "WHAT! THEY DID WHAT?" "I am sorry ma'am. This will not happen again." Aunt Mary hung up the phone and demanded for all of us to come in the hallway. She was determined to find out which one of us was cursing the woman out on the phone. They all pointed at me. She whipped all of us. Tamera was mad at us because she did not do anything, but she received a whipping.

The next morning, Granny came home from the hospital. She told Momma that they think that she might need a pacemaker because her heart kept skipping beats. Momma called the physician and he said the same thing. The physician said that Granny needed to see Dr. Jackson in Little Rock. Momma asked, "How can I find Dr. Jackson?" The physician replied, "I'm not sure but call the New Baptist Hospital." Momma told the physician that she would.

The next day, Momma called around to find some local doctors, so she could get a second opinion. Momma was calling every doctor's office in Camden to get a second opinion. They all suggested Dr. Jackson in Little Rock. She got upset, but she did not want Granny to know, so she asked Hershey to come to the house to sit with Granny for about an hour. She explained to him what was going on and he showed up immediately. Aunt Mary Helen came too. She told Momma by the time she was to the house she would be gone because her job would not allow her to take anymore days. Momma acted as if she understood.

Momma and I walked downtown. We were about three houses down from Betsy house. It had been several days since I saw Betsy. We were in front of Ms. Mary Bell's house. Momma and I smelled a strong stench. The closer we got to Betsy's house the stronger the odor became. It was something dead, somewhere close. Betsy was standing in the door and saw us coming down the street. She burst out the door, ran, and hugged me. She told me how much she had missed me. I shared the mutual feelings. Betsy asked, "Do you want to see a dead nigger?" I told her no. She pulled me to the shed that still had covers hanging on it, and then the flashback came back to my head. We had made it to the opening of the shed. Betsy put her hand on the cover and I took off running toward Momma. Momma and Mrs. Ann was exchanging address for Betsy and me. I told Momma I was ready to go and Betsy was laughing at me. She told me I had better not tell anyone or her daddy would find me. A couple more weeks went by and it was time to go back to school.

I remember my first day at Whiteside School. It was on the white side of town. It was 1975; I was in the third grade. I went into the bathroom at lunchtime. It was recess and some of the girls came in the bathroom. They were talking about Bloody Mary. I asked who was Bloody Mary, and then one of the girls told me that Bloody Mary was an old, mean woman that died. The girl also said that Bloody Mary did not like it when you called her name. Two of the girls were in the mirror looking at their reflection in the mirror. One of the girls said, "On the count of three we can do it together." The little girl and me looked at each and got quiet. Then we turned our attention towards the girls that were in the mirror. The two girls knocked on the mirror three times and then called Bloody Mary's name three times. They stepped back, laughed, and asked who was next. One of the girls looked at me and said, "It's your turn!" I said, "NO! I don't think so!" She looked at the little girl on the side of me and asked her. The little girl shook her head no. The other girl that was with her said, "Why are you all so scared? It is just a joke. You all need to stop being babies." She laughed at us and we all walked out the bathroom. The school bell rang and it was time to go back to class. Before I knew it, the last bell of the day rang and school was over. I felt important because I had a group of new friends. We met in the open hallways after school. We introduced ourselves. Jennifer, Terrie and Better were the girls that knocked on the mirror in the bathroom during lunch. Deloris was the girl in bathroom that stood on my side, but everyone called her DD. We were walking to the bus stop so we could go home and Terrie said she had to use the bathroom. We were walking and talking about what had happened in the bath earlier. We had a pact that said we would not tell a soul about what we had did in the bathroom. Since we were all new best friends, we decided we would do everything together. We all entered into the dark bathroom. Terrie let out a big scream. She pointed toward the bathroom sinks where they had played Bloody Mary. We looked at her and started laughing. Jennifer said, "Look Bloody Mary were here and she ran out the bathroom. Tonya, DD, and I looked at the sink, and both sinks were covered in blood. There were footprints of blood on the floor. We all froze in our tracks. All three of our eyes roamed and examined the room. At the same time, our feet were moving backwards out that bathroom. Then we took off to the bus stop and the teacher on duty asked us what was wrong. We all said nothing at the same time.

We walked over to Terrie because she was throwing up. We wanted to check on her. The teacher walked to us and asked what bus line we were supposed to be in. We all went into our book bags and pulled the bus schedule out. I said I had green line. DD had green line too. Jennifer, Terrie and Tonya had red line. She told us to go to our lines and she would take care of Terrie. DD and I told them goodbye and we both told Terrie we hope she felt better soon. DD took my hand and we walked to our line.

All of the buses were running late, so DD and I played in our bus line. We were having a good time. I heard a little boy say, "That's Witchy Poops' daughter." I started to cry. I could not believe that they were still calling me names. I was so embarrassed and did not know what to do, but cry. DD said, "That's my friend. Don't talk about her." She wanted to know who said it, but no one answered. I felt better because I finally had a friend who would take up for me. The bus came and the little boy got on it. I could not wait to get home and tell Momma about what happened. The bus came to a stop and I started to get off. I was walking off the bus and I heard DD say wait up, this is my stop too. I was too happy to find out that we had the same stop. We got off the bus together and she asked me for my phone number. We exchanged number and she walked home with her boyfriend, Dewayne. As time flew by, we became close friends.

What Goes On In Momma's Closet

The summer was here again and Granny grew sicker. Momma decided to take a trip to Little Rock to check out some heart doctors. Jean picked us up at the bus station. Momma called around and set up an appointment with a heart doctor. Dr. Lewis's Office was right in front of the State Capital Offices. Momma had her doctor appointment lined up, so now she had to find a house. She called a realtor to find a house. The real estate agent came right out. Mr. Jim, the real estate agent, was a nice, pleasant understanding man. He found Momma a house on 15th and Abigail. It was a little white house on the corner, deep in the west end of Little Rock. The next morning, Jean dropped us off at the Greyhound bus stop. We headed back to Camden. I realized that if we left Camden that meant I would have to leave my friend, DD. I was not happy about that at all. I shared that with my Momma. She said that she understood that, but I was not the only one who was going to lose out. She explained that she was giving up her house and private business, which she built up from the ground. She asked me what was more important, Grandma or my friends. I did not answer that question. Momma then said, "Grandma Eleanor needs a pace maker to help her heart beat. If she does not get it, she will die. In Little Rock, Doctor Jackson is the only one in the State of Arkansas that can do it. I will tell you what, we can go by all of your friend's houses and get their address and you can write them." We walked to all of my friend's houses. She made sure that she had all of the correct addresses. Momma told me that we were not moving yet because they were still running tests on Granny. She said she could have an answer by tomorrow around ten o'clock because Granny had to go back to the doctor, and the results should be back. We walked to K.F.C and picked up a bucket of chicken, then headed home.

We finally made it home. Granny, a pale color, was sitting in the living room. She told Momma that she was tired. Momma fixed everyone a small plate. While we were eating, I could not help but to stare at Granny. She looked weak and she was still tired. I could not believe how weak she was. This was the same Granny that could shoot a snake out of a tree from a block away. We finished eating and Momma helped Granny get into bed.

The next morning, Momma took me to the doctor with them. The news was not good. At that moment, Momma made her decision that we were moving to Little Rock. Granny was upset because she did not like changes. I remember them fussing about Momma and her prayers. Granny said, "You prayed for all those other people and they where healed. Why can't you pray for me and I will be healed?" Momma explained to her that she did pray when she was in the hospital. She told Granny that she would be okay. Granny did not want to hear that. She did not believe Momma had prayed for her. Momma told her again that she did pray for her and that she has to have faith. Granny needed to pray for herself too. Granny started to lose her faith in God. She wanted everyone to give up his or her faith too. Every day, Momma and Granny would have a big fight. I was going to the bus stop, about a block down from the house, and I could still hear them fighting. It seemed like I was still in the house. The kids were laughing at me. I was very embarrassed. I put my head down and cried. I heard DD ask me what was wrong. She grabbed me and hugged me. I heard a male voice say, "Witchy Poo 1 and Witchy Poo 2 are arguing because Witchy Poo 2 forgot to put the broom back after she rode it." All the kids laughed at me. Even DD smirked. Then she said, "You better leave my friend along unless you want to fight me." Everyone got quiet. They all stopped laughing. The bus came and we got in and headed to school. After school, I went into the house and Momma was packing up everything in the house. I asked her were we moving to Little Rock. She replied saying, "Yes." I was ready to move at that point, because I realized I could start over there since no one knew me. I told Momma about the kids picking on me because she and Granny were always fighting. I told her that I wanted to move so I could start over with new friends. She laughed and said, "You got that right. Some of the people in the town told me that I was not a healer because Momma would be healed by now. Yes, Maria it is time to start over.

God is the only friend you will need. Let us make time for him. Okay?" I said okay. She said, "It sounds like prayer time. He is waiting for us to speak, to move, to act out faith. The ministry of the Holy Spirit is revealed in the names ascribed to Him, Comforter, Counselor, Helper, Advocate, Intercessor, Strengthener, Standby (John 16:7). Faith means being sure of the things we hope for and knowing that something is real even if we do not see it. It is by faith we understand that the whole world was made by God's command, so what we see was made by something that cannot be seen. Without faith, no one can please God. Anyone who comes to God must believe that he is real and there will be rewards to those who truly want to find him. (Hebrews 11:1, 3, 6). Right now Maria, we are going to make a commitment to trust God, okay?" I told Momma okay. Momma continued saying, "Because you are faithful and trustworthy, I make a commitment to trust in you with all my heart and lean not on my understanding; in all my paths straight. I am blessed, for I trust in the Lord, in whom I put my confidence. Amen." I said Amen. By the time we got through packing up all our things, it was late. We ate and went to bed.

4

LEARNING TO PUT GOD FIRST

THE NEXT MORNING, the mover was there to pick up the furniture. Herman and Jay were in his bedroom talking. I stood in the bathroom door and listened to them talk. James asked what to do. Herman replied, "Right do what? Call the police and tell them what! That scar face pulled a gun on us and then he raped us. What do you think that the police will say? Its two big boys and you all couldn't protect yourselves from that one man?" Jay said, "Man, I guess you are right. We are only twelve and thirteen years old and he is like a 30 years old. Can you believe it's already 1976? Herman when do you think that we will see each another again?" "I am not sure Jay." "Well I am going to miss you man. I just wanted to tell you bye." Bump! "Hey Herman, what's that noise?" My eyes got big. I grabbed my mouth. I was scared. I knew if Herman knew I was listening to them talk he would hurt me. I walked to the sink and played like I was washing my hands. Herman walked back to the bedroom. "Naw, I don't think she heard us." Jay blew out a deep breath. I wanted to tell him that I saw scar face hanging in Betsy shed.

Aunt Daisy came to the house to pick Herman and me up so we would not be in the way. A few hours later, we went back to the house and it was empty. All the furniture was on the truck. We took a taxi to Little Rock, Arkansas. Somehow, we beat the moving company there. Momma, Herman, and I slept in a hotel. We finally settled in our house on 15th and Abigail. A few weeks later it was time to go back to school.

It was 1976, and I was in the 4th grade. Momma walked me to school and registered me into Stephen's Elementary School. After the registration, she walked me to my classroom. I walked into the classroom I only saw a few kids in there. I breathed out nice and gentle. I saw a man walk towards Momma. I thought that it was one on the kid's parents. He reached his hands out to Momma and said, "I am Mr. Carpenter. I will be the teacher in this fourth grade classroom this year. I am looking forward to working with you. Is this Maria?" Momma said, "Yes, this is Maria." Momma told me goodbye and my heart sped up a few beats. I was very scared and I could not move. Mr. Carpenter took my arm and said in a gentle voice, "Let me show you where you will sit." I nodded my head and walked with him. He put me in the front of the classroom. Later on, the new kids started coming into the classroom. Before long, all of the empty seats were full. The bell had rung and it was the first recess. A tall, skinny girl walked up to me and said her name was Jennifer, and then she asked if I wanted to play with her. I told her my name was Maria and I would love to play with her, so we walked to the playground. Some girls were jumping rope and told Jenifer to come hold the jump rope. I sat down on the ground and watched them jump rope. A little girl walked up to me and said her name was Donna Lee. She wanted me to play tetherball with her. I told her I had never played before. Donna told me to come on and she will show me how to play. I went with her and she showed me. The bell rang and it was time to go back into the school. We lined up by classrooms.

We made it back into the classroom and Mr. Carpenter said, "Finally everyone is here, let us introduce ourselves." He started with himself. He said, "My name is Mr. Carpenter. I was born in West Africa. I will be your teacher for the year." Before he could finish his sentence, a little boy raised his hand. Mr. Carpenter said, "Do you want to go first?" The little boy said, "No. I have a question to ask you sir?" Mr. Carpenter said, "Okay, what do you want to ask me?" The boy said, "You are white! How are you from West

Africa?" The other kids said all around the same time, "Yes. We want to know that too." He smiled and said, "Kids there are white people in Africa too." Everyone was shocked. Mr. Carpenter broke the shock mode and grabbed our attention again by asking the little boy to start introducing himself and tell what he wanted to be when he grew up. The little boy said, "Tyrone Wilson, and I want to be a doctor." The rest of the kids followed by introducing themselves and telling what they wanted to be when they grew up. Before long, the last bell of the day rang. Jennifer and I walked out of the classroom together. She wanted to know which way I walked home. I told her that I walked to the west, behind the school, to get home. She was upset because she had to walk east to go home. We told each other goodbye. I told her I would see her tomorrow at school. She said, "Okay." We waved goodbye. I started walking toward my way home, then I heard, "Wait up!" It was Donna running towards me. She asked me which way I stayed. I told her 15th and Abigail. She smiled and said, "I stay right around the corner. I stay on 11th and Peyton. We can walk home together every day." I was happy I had a friend.

I ran into the house to tell Momma, but Granny said she was at work. I said, "Momma got a job?" Granny smile and said, "Yes. Now what do you want to eat?" I told her chicken noodle soup. While she prepared my food, I told her about my new friend. She said, "I saw that little girl and it's something about her that I just don't like." I dropped my head and said to myself, "You don't like anybody." I finished eating and went outside to play alone. Granny called me back in the house and told me to take off my school clothes. I headed back outside, and by the time I opened the door, Donna was about to knock on the door. We smiled and I walked outside. She told me come and walk with her, so that I would know where she live. We walked three blocks down the street and we were at her house. I played with her for a few minutes and then I went back home.

As the months passed by, Donna and my friendship grew and we became good friends. Six months later, it was almost time for school to end. After school, on the walk home, Donna and I were talking about how fast the school year had passed by. Donna told me that her Momma was looking for a house in a neighborhood on the Eastside of Little Rock. She was upset about it because that meant that we were not going to be in the same school for the next year. We finally made it to my house. Donna wanted me to go over her house after school because she wanted me to meet her cousin Joyce Moore who stayed next door to her. I told Donna to hold on and let me go and put my homework up. She said, "Okay." She waited outside for me. I told Granny that I would be right back. Granny told me, "Don't let the street lights catch you, because that will be your butt!" I rolled my eyes and replied, "Okay." Then I walked out the door. We walked over to Donna's house and met Joyce. We played for a few minutes and then I went back to the house.

One day after school, I was at home in my front yard playing. This little girl was walking down my street. She looked around and saw me. I ran and jumped into the tree. The little girl walked into my yard and stood under the tree that I had jumped into. She said, "My name is Sherry Minor. What is your name?" I was still sitting in the tree and I looked down at her and said, "my name is Maria." Sherry demanded that I come down out the tree and talk to her. I jumped down from the tree and we talked. I really enjoyed talking to her. She taught me about boys and parties. She told me things that I did not even know existed. Sherry opened up my mind to a completely new world. She started coming over more and more, and our friendship took on a whole new meaning.

Momma finally had a day off, so she asked me if I wanted to go to the store. I said yes. We walked out the house and went down a big hill. Two blocks later, we were on 13th and Abigail. A little girl walked up to Momma and asked her if I could play with her sometime. Momma said, "What is your name? The girl said, "My name is Tina Gaines, and we just moved into this house. I don't have any friends over here yet." Momma told her that we were going to the store and after we left, I could come back and play with her. Tina said, "Okay." Momma told her to go get her mom and ask if it was okay for her to have a friend over to play with her. Tina ran in the house and got her mom, Lily Gaines. Lily and Momma introduced themselves to each other. Tina and I got to know each other too. Momma and I headed off to the store. Momma looked up and said, "There is my co-worker, Barbara. Let's go up there so you can meet her." We were on 13th and Abigail and we walked up one long block, which looked like it should have been two blocks. We crossed the street and then we were on 13th and Lewis. Ms. Barbara's house was right on the corner. She was in front of her house. Mrs. Barbara said, "Hello, I have a daughter that is as big as you. Her name is Pam." She called Pam outside and introduced us to each other. Pam wanted to play with me but Momma told her that I had to come back another day to play with her. We all said goodbye. We walked to the store. Momma said, "You have a lot of new friends." I said I sure do. I was so happy. We headed back home from the store. While Momma put up the things that we had bought at the store, I asked if I could go out and play with Tina. She told me to go ahead and not stay to long. I said, "Okay Momma." I walked down the hill to her house. Tina and I sat on her porch and talked for a while. Joyce walked down to Tina's house and said, "What are you doing over here? Donna is going to get you." I asked Tina, "What did she think was going on." Tina said, "They are crazy." I did not think any more about it. I left Tina's house and went home so I could take a bath and get ready for school the next day.

I walked out the door and did not see Donna. I thought to myself, that was awkward, because normally Donna would be outside or coming down the street so we could walk to school together. I went on and walked to school alone. "Morning class. My name is Mr. Carpenter, and I will your six grader teacher." "But you are a man. How are you a teacher?" "What? Who said that?" A dark skinned little boy stood up out his seat. He straighten up his head and poked out his chest and said, I said that." "Mr. Carpenter said, "What is your name?" "I am Willie Williams." "Mr. Williams said, I am a male and I am also a teacher. This is 1977 and times have changed. We now have men that are teacher." "Are you one of those funny teachers?" The classroom started laughing. Mr. Carpenter became a little frustrated and said, "Mr. Williams I see that you will be the class clown this year. I just wonder if I called your mother and asked her how she feels about her son being the class clown, I wonder would she be just as tickle as you." "Hold on Mr. Carpenter, there is no need to call her. I will behaved." The class started laughing again. "Okay, You all that's enough. Now I will finished what I started to say. Yes, I am a male teacher, but what you all did not know is that I am from West Africa." The class got quit. It was so quiet until you could have heard a pin drop. "Okay, Mr.

What Goes On In Momma's Closet

Carpenter, I tried to be quiet, but you are white. Everyone's knows that black folks are from Africa." The whole classroom agreed with him. Mr. Carpenter said while he were laughing, "We have a lot to learn this year.

Before I knew it, it was lunchtime. I ate and went outside. I sat down alone and I watched all the kids having fun on the playground. Everyone was having fun, but me. I heard Donna walk up behind me and say, "Aw now! Why didn't you wait for me? You think you're too good to walk with me to school?" I told her. "I looked for you and you weren't there like you normally are." She said, "Are you getting smart with me?" I said, "No." She was talking so loud until it got some of the kids' attention that was playing next to us. The children came closer to hear what was going on. Donna really showed out then. She said, "After school, I am going to beat you up!" I told her I did not want to fight her. I said, "I thought that you were my friend?" She said, "I was until I saw you playing with that girl, Tina. I do not like her and you cannot play with her if you are going to be my friend. That is why I am going to get you after school." After school, I saw a group of kids walking behind me. They were all really loud. I could hear them laughing and talking about me. They were calling me a friend trader and they were telling Donna to get me good. Four blocks from the school, I heard all the kids running behind me. My heart was racing a hundred miles per hour. All of the sudden I felt someone pull me to the ground. Donna jumped on top of me and sat down on my body. She started hitting me. All I could do was to cry. I did not understand why she was hitting me and pulling my hair. I just laid there and took it. The kids was just laughing and talking about me. Donna yelled, "Why aren't you fighting me back?" I told her, "I don't know how." I had never had a fight before. I was still crying. I could not believe my best friend was hurting me like that. She got up from off the top of my body and told me that she was sorry. The kids started walking off and I heard someone call her weak. We walked off. She asked me, "Why I couldn't fight." I told her that I haven't been around people like her. She said that she was going to teach me how to fight. I finally made it home. I knew I did not want to play with her again. I was glad school was over in a few days. Later that day she came to the house and I told my granny to tell her that I was not home. The next day she knocked on the door so that we could walk to school together. I walked to school and felt like it was my longest walk that I had ever had. I was glad there were only two days left in school.

School finally ended. I decided to go to Tina's house and play with her. Tina and I were on her front porch talking when Sherry walked by and saw me. Then she asked Tina if she could come in and talk with us. Tina invited her in. We all were on the front porch having a good time.

The next day we did the same thing and met back on Tina's porch. Donna and Joyce walked up to Tina's fence at her house and Donna told me to come out. I said, "No I'm not going outside the fence to talk to you." She said, "Then, I am going to wait for you to go home and then I am going to get you again." Tina and Sherry told them to get away from the fence with that mess. Donna and Joyce walked away from the fence, but that didn't go quietly. Joyce told Donna, "Don't worry, we will get Maria." One hour later, we were still having fun. I decided that I had enough fun for the day and I was going to go home. I walked out the gate of Tina's house and I passed the corner of Tina's house. There was an alley right on the side of her house. The alley lead to Donna's and Joyce's house. I peeked down the alley and saw Donna and Joyce standing in the middle of the alley. They had stood there hours just waiting for me to come out. I walked back around the corner of Tina's house and back in the gate, and I sat down on the porch of her house. All I could do was cry. Tina and Sherry asked, "What did you do to her to make her so upset?" I told them that Donna said that if I did not stop talking to Tina I wasn't her friend, because she didn't like her. Tina said, "Then she needs to be upset with me instead of you." Sherry and I agreed with Tina, but it did not change the fact that she wanted to fight me. Donna finally moved to the other side of town.

One year later, Momma started picking up more jobs, so I barely saw her. It was 1978; school was getting ready to start again. The party of the year was coming up. The flash party that everyone wanted to attend. Sherry and I had walked all over town just having fun. She was very resourceful when it came to money. She could not find money anywhere. I knew as long as I was with her she would find a way for us to eat. That whole day, she was telling me how much fun we would have if we could get the money to go. We did not have any luck finding money, so we gave up and went home. I walked through my door, went into the bathroom, and took a shower. Before I could get my clothes on, I heard the phone ring. My gut told me it was Sherry and she found the money so we could go to the party of the year. Momma called me to the phone. I threw a towel on my body and got the phone. "Maria are you dressed." I told her no. She said, "Well get dressed because we are going to the party." I said, "For real?" She said, "Hurry up and get dressed, then call me back." I hung up the phone and quickly put on my clothes. Momma asked me, "Why are you putting on fresh clothes and its 7 pm. It's time for you to get in the bed." I told her that I was trying them on to see how my new shorts fit. She said okay. Then she walked out of my bedroom and sat down in the living room. I went in to check on her and she was sleep. I picked up the phone and called Sherry to tell her to meet me because I was ready. Sherry told me to meet her at 14th and Lewis Street I said okay and hung up the phone. I tip toed to the door. I heard my Granny say, "Hey where are you going? I know you didn't let that little devil Sherry Minor talk you into sneaking out the house?" I said, "No, granny." I walked out the house. I took off running. Two blocks later, I was at 14th and Lewis. I looked for Sherry and I did not see her. I stood there for a minute and I still did not see her. I decided to go home. Before I could step off the curb, a car pulled up. I saw Sherry sitting in the front seat of the car. She opened the door and said, "Get in sugar. We are going to the party of the year." My eyes lit up. I stepped into the car and said hello to the woman that was driving the car. The woman said, "Hello my name is Ms. Jackson. What is yours?" I told her Maria and I said thanks for giving us a ride. She said, "You are welcome. You are nice. Why are you hanging with Sherry?" We all laughed and Sherry heard her favorite song, Flash light, come on. Sherry turned up the radio, and we all started singing along with the song. Then I remembered word for word what Sherry had said about what would go on at the party. I daydreamed all the way there. I thought about all of the music, food, dancing, and the stroll lights with different colors moving in circular motion. When I opened up my eyes, we were on West 12th and Van Buren Street. The woman that was driving the car made a right turn. While she was making the turn, she told us to be careful because the night did not have any eyes. This was my very first party. The woman drove to the top of the hill and we were at War Memorial Swimming Pool. Sherry jumped out the car and folded the seat frontward so that I could climb out of the back seat. As I was getting out, I told Mrs. Jackson thanks for the ride. Sherry said, "Oh yeah, how much do I owe you?" Mrs. Jackson laughed and said, "You are welcome Maria and Sherry you have to babysit for me, okay?" Sherry said, "Okay." Sherry shut the car door, then we walked to the top of the steps. Mrs. Jackson drove off. Sherry said, "I am not babysitting them bad kids." We laughed, and Sherry handed our money to the woman at the admissions booth. We walked into the party. My eyes got big from all of the things that I saw. It was a beautiful color coming from the stroll lights. We were in the pool swinging and dancing. Other people were on the sides of the pool dancing. All you could hear was people laughing and having a good time. I smelled barbeque food coming from the grill. I was amazed at all the different activities going on. The party was everything that she said it would be. I jumped from the ball that was coming in my direction. I heard someone say, "I am sorry for that." Then I saw Donna jump out the pool to get the ball. She grabbed the ball and said, "Maria, I miss you so much. I am sorry for everything." I looked up and saw Sherry on the dance floor with a cute guy. Donna looked and saw that I looked up at Sherry. She said, "Come on, get in the water, and play volleyball with us." Before I could say okay, she was pulling me into the water. We both jumped in the pool. I played volleyball until I could not see straight.

The music

I had the best time of my life. Sherry danced the whole time. Before long, the party was over and It was time to leave. Sherry caught up with me so we could leave. We walked out of the party and walked down the steps. I saw Donna getting in the car. Donna looked up at me, jumped out of her car, grabbed me by the hand and told me to come and get into the car. I asked her what about Sherry. She said that they did not have room for her. The car was filled up. Sherry said, "You better not get into that car, because I would never leave you like that." I told Donna, "That's ok; I'm going to walk home with Sherry." Donna made her mom ask me to ride home with them. Her mom begged me to get into the car. I told her that I had to walk home with Sherry. She said fine, and told Donna that it was not anything she could do about it. Sherry had proceeded to walk across the street and then she called me to come. I told Donna's mom thanks for the offer. I really wanted that ride because I was tired. Sherry said, "I know you weren't thinking about leaving me like that were you?" I said, "No

Sherry, I would never leave you." We walked down the big hill. We were still talking about all the fun that we had. Sherry was always so hilarious when she talked about people. She could make anyone laugh. We were laughing so hard that both of us were crying tears of joy. We were on our way home, walking across the bridge, when I heard someone call Sherry's name. I said, "Sherry, someone is calling your name." She said, "Don't pay them any attention." We kept laughing and walking. Then I realized that it was completely dark. Normally I would be in the house at this time of night. I thought about my Momma and I knew that she was probably pacing back and forth worrying about me. I knew that Granny was blaming everything on Sherry Minor. I knew that I was going to get in trouble for being out too late. We were heading into complete darkness. I started getting even more scared because it was too dark. A normal person should be in the house. The more I thought about it, the more I realize that it was too dark for me to be out. Down the hill we went. I heard some man calling Sherry's name. The man said, "I know you hear me calling your name." I heard footsteps running behind us. It sounded like it was getting closer to us. My heart started beating fast. I heard men voices saying, "Y'all need to STOP." The steps of horses started getting closer. I knew then something wasn't right, but I just didn't know what it was. I looked back behind us. I said, "Sherry some guys are running behind us." Sherry said, "RUN!" I said, "What? What for? I am tired." Before all the words could come out my mouth, Sherry was halfway down the block. It was completely dark, and I was all alone. I knew that it was time to run. I took off, but it was too late. A man had grabbed my arm. Another took off behind Sherry. He said, "Which way did your buddy go?" I said, "I don't know. It's too dark to see." I asked him to let go of my arm he said, "No, but if LG catches Sherry I will let you go." LG came back empty handed. I snatched my arm and took off running for my life. One block later he caught me again. He and LG were out of breath. It did not stop them from pulling me back to his house. I told him that I did not want to go into his house. I was screaming and howling to the top of my lungs. He put his salted hands over my mouth. I bit him then he slapped me to the ground. He pulled me up the steps that lead to his bedroom. He then pulled me back out of the bedroom door, to the total darkness of his back yard. He told LG to hold me until he could go and shut his door. LG grabbed me very tight. I tried to get a loose. I broke free only to be caught by LG. LG pulled my body back to the yard. I heard a voice say LG where are you? He said, "Willie I am right here." Willie said, "Damn man. I thought you decided to keep this one for yourself." He said, "No Willie I would not do you like that." Willie said, "Debra is in the house. I had to go and turn my radio up." Willie grabbed me and took me back up the three steps to his room's back door. He put his hands on my mouth. He turned around and told LG to watch out for him. He said I am going first and next will be your turn. I did not know what turn they meant but I knew it was not good. I wiggled and tried to get loose. He dropped his hand from my mouth and I screamed as loud as I could. I howled and screamed in hope that someone would hear and help me. I heard, Debra, his sister knocking on the door. "Willie, what are you doing in there? Who is that you have in there?" He threw me on the twin-sized bed. Then climbed on top of me, slapped me and then put his hand over my mouth. Willie said, "If you scream again I am going to hurt you. Do you understand that?" I nodded my head. He removed his hand from my mouth. I asked him why he was doing this to me. Willie replied by saying, "Sherry borrowed five dollars from me. She said that you all were hungry. I told her that she could use the money to feed you all, but she would have to give me my money back, and if she could not pay me my money back, then she would have to give me some cat. Since she ran from me, I could not catch her, but now I have you. You will have to do. I said, "But Mr., I didn't take your money from you. Please do not hurt me, sir. Please I did not do anything to you." He said, "Someone has to give me my money's worth. I burst my butt washing dishes. I worked too hard for my money." He pulled my pants down and I pulled my pants back up. I kept begging him to stop. We kept playing tug of war with my pants. I said, "Please stop." His bedspread was full of water from my tears. I bawled as he shredded my shorts off my bottom. His sister came back to the door beating on the door. I yelled, "Help me please!" The music was so loud. He laid in between my thighs, and I felt him ripping my private part a loose. I was in so much pain. All I could do was feel him in my secret closet door. He kept forcing himself in my personal part. The pain was so intense. It felt like fire inside of me. I squeal out from the pain. I could barely hear his sister beating on the door. The pain was more than my body could take. The last thing I remembered him saying was to be still and it won't hurt you so much.

I woke up to him pulling me off the bed. He said wake up and come on. He opened the door and gave LG a high five. He told LG how tight my body was. LG said. "Man you ripped her apart. It's my turn now." "No man, we have to go because Debra said she was calling the police. Let's go man." Willie shut his bathroom door. I felt some dripping down from my private part. I then saw a woman come from the front part of the house. LG and Willie froze. I was so scared. My mind told me to run and that is what I did. I took off. Debra was still talking to them and I got a good head start. I ran three blocks down the street and then I heard them running behind me. I jumped into a deep ditch. I hid under a bridge that went over the ditch. I heard them walking over the bridge that I was hiding under. I sat my bottom on the concrete then I jumped up because of the pain that I still felt in my bottom. I laid on my side so it wouldn't hurt as bad. The needier pains of fire keep shooting up from my private part all the way up to my stomach. The pain took over my body. The drama scene kept replaying in my head. The pain was so intense that I passed out. I woke up to footsteps walking over my head. I heard their voices and I put my hands over my mouth to keep from screening. I heard LG say, "Man I didn't even get my turn. That's messed up." Willie said, "That's not my fault. That was Debra's nosey butt." LG said, "Man we have looked for her for over an hour. I am tired and I am going home. Her pussy isn't that important. I will see you tomorrow." They said their goodnights. I peeked from under the bridge and waited until they disappeared. Then, I slowly climbed up from under the bridge. I peeked out very slow, trying not to make any noises. I looked up at the street and I did not see signs that were still in the area, so I jumped up and took off. I saw a street sign that read "Green Mountain Drive." I knew I had a long walk to get to the house. The wind had picked up. It was blowing the trees and paper all over the street. Every time I heard a noise, I would take off running. Whenever I stopped running, the memory was still replaying in my mind. It was a car in sight on the streets. My mind played so many tricks on me, so I jumped into some bushes. I was not sure if one of them had gotten into a car and was searching for me. Another car came by and I hid behind another bush. I peeked out slowly and saw that it was a police car. By that time I had made it home, I was a vegetable.

I knocked on the door. Grandma Eleanor opened up the door and her mouth dropped. I stepped into the house and fell on the floor. I could not make it any further. I wanted to get up off the floor, but my bottom was numb. All that I could do was just lay there and let the memories flood in my mind again. I heard Momma talking on the phone to someone. Next thing I remember is the police saying, "Don't touch her body. Just grab her hand and tell her that you love her." He was so upset that he had to walk off. I heard him talking to his partner on the porch. He said, "What kind of monster could do this to a kid? Damn, she looks like she is only 12 years old. She is the same age of my daughter. Did you see the way her short was ripped off her and they were all pulled apart?" The other cop said, "Man that's a lot of blood on her." I felt my lifeless body being picked up. I went back out and I felt a bump as they were taking my body down the steps to the ambulance. My eyes opened up to the police. The officer said, "Don't worry; I will give you my word that I will stay out here until we catch him. If I have to work two shifts, then that is what I am going to do." I looked up at him into his pretty, brownish eyes, and said thank you. The paramedics pushed me into the ambulance and shut the door. The man that was working on me tried not to look at me because his eyes were full of tears. He told my Momma that he has saw many things, but nothing touched him like this. Momma had just shut down. She was numb. She never said a word all the way to the hospital.

About five minutes later, we were at the hospital. Nurses and the doctor were at the emergency room doors. They were ready for me because the first response driver had already called in to the emergency team so that they could prepare for me. Once we made it into the hospital, the team was in place. They were greeting us. Then they took over. I was pushed back into a room. I was still in a daze. The memories were still fresh in my mind. I could still hear Willie in my head saying, "be quiet." It was as if he was still there. My mind zoomed back out because the nurse said, "Hello? Hello? Can you hear me? I am talking to you." I jumped and crawled up in the corner of the bed. I just wanted to go home and get into my bed. I never said a word to her. All I could do was cry and listen to his voice over in my head. The doctor walked in the room and looked at me. I was still in the corner of the bed. I was so scared. He walked closer to me. I said please do not hurt me anymore. He told the nurse that I needed a minute. He walked back out the room. Momma just sat in the corner with her eyes full of water. If she blinked her eyes, tears would fall. A few minutes later, the doctor came back in the room. He said, "Ma'am I am sorry for what that man did, but I need to check your bottom to see how much damage has been done to you. I need you to be a big girl for me. Your mom will be right here the whole time. I need you to come out that corner and lay down on the bed." I crawled tighter in the corner because that is what Willie had told me to do. Momma stood up with tears in her eyes, looked me in my eyes, and said, "Maria. The doctor can't help you until you do what he asked you to do." The tears were rolling down her face. I finally listened to her and the doctor told and showed me everything he was doing and everything that he had to use before he touch me with it. My body was still pretty sore and tender. I tried my best to be still, but I was still having many pains. Every time I jumped, his eyes watered up. Finally, the process was over. He got up and said, "That son of B. Someone needs to be hanged." He walked out the door mad. The nurse apologized for his behavior. They said that it is not like him. Momma told them that it was okay. The nurses went and found me some clothes because Willie had ripped up my clothes, and plus, they needed it for evidence. I did not understand what that meant. The nurse walked back in the room with a dress that I could wear home. Someone knock on the door. The nurse told Momma that it was a detective. They needed to asked me some questions. Momma told them to come in. The police officer said hello to me. Then he said, "You are lucky because you have a police officer willing to give up their free time to catch the guy who did this to you. Now, I need you to tell me what happen to you. I need you to try to remember everything, and tell me word for word what happen to you." I was happy that I had a police offer willing to give up their free time for me. I told him, word for word, what happen to me. The detective asked me did I remember where Willie house was, and I told him yes. He asked me have I ever ridden in a police car before, and I told him no. He said, "You and your mom will be riding home in one tonight, but first I need you to show me where Willie lives. I jumped in the corner and told him, "No. Willie said that he would hurt me. I never want to go by there again." I just stood in the corner and cried. The memories were back in my head. One of the officers walked out the room. The detective walked to the corner where I balled up in the corner, and he grabbed my head and made me look up. He showed me his gun and said, "I will not let that man hurt you, or anyone else ever again. He is going to jail for a long time. That is, if you show me where he lives. Do you want him to do this to another little girl?" I said no. Momma and I walked off with the police officer, and we got into his car. I showed him where Willie lived. We parked in front of

What Goes On In Momma's Closet

Willie's house and the detective called on his radio for back up police officers to come to the address. Within minutes, gangs of police officers were there. We drove off, and he took us home. I was glad to pull up to the house. I took a bath and fell asleep in the bathtub.

I woke up the next morning in my bed. Momma said, "I can't believe that I haven't been spending anytime with you. I had been working so hard to pay all these bills. I am going to spend some time with you. I know what the problem is." I said, "What is it?" Momma said, "We need to make time for God." Momma said, "We are going to pray right now. God please forgive us from our sin." Then she picked up her bible and turned to John 15; 1–6.

1. I am the true vine, and my Father is the husband. 2. Every branch in me that beareth not fruit, he take away; and every branch that beareth fruit, he poureth it that it may bring forth more fruit. 3. Now, ye are clean through the word, which I have spoken unto you. 4. Abide in me, and I in you. As the branch cannot bear fruit of itself, except it abide in the vine; no more can ye, except ye abide in me. 5. I am the vine, ye are the branches: He that abideth in me, and I in him, the same bringeth forth much fruit for without me ye can do nothing. 6. If a man abide not in me, he is cast forth as a branch, and is withered; and men gather them, cast them into fire, and they are burned.

Matthew 7:18

18. A good tree cannot bring forth evil fruit; neither can a corrupt tree bring forth good fruit.

Closet Prayers

The message that I get is loud and clear; PUT GOD FIRST, and everything else will be added unto you. If he takes it away from you, it is only because it will not bring you good fruit.

We need to look down the road sometimes. Make a list, put good on the right side of your list and bad on the left side. If the bad outweighs the good, then you already know what time it is.

I know how easy it is to hold on to the bad side. I understand how hard it is to let go and let God take over the problem.

I know that it is easy to tell someone else to let go and let the Lord handle it, but when it came to me, it was so hard to let things go. When you do not let go of things after you pray about it, you are sending God a negative message.

You know He created the heavens and the earth. You know He has great powers, but if you are taking the problem back out of his hand, it shows that you lack in faith.

What kind of message do you want to send Him? The Bible tells us, repeatedly, that He loves it when we have faith. When my faith is not where it supposed to be, or when I'm in something that is over my head, that is when I go to my closet.

This is the message that I want to send him. "Father I will trust you. I know you are God and I know that you are in control. I am not sure how you are going to fix it but I am going to trust you. I am trying to stop taking this out of your hands Lord, but I am weak. Lord please help me. Amen."

Momma's prayers always had a way of relaxing my weary soul. I know that Momma had a special type of a relationship God. I knew if she prayed, everything would be all right.

Momma told me that she was waiting for a call from Annette Fisher. The phone rang the minute she said that. She and Mrs. Annette talked for a few minutes. Then they hung up the phone, and Momma told me to pack up the books that I wanted to take to Mrs. Fisher house. I packed everything up. A few minutes later, Mrs. Annette came and picked us up. We went to her house while Momma did some work for her. I sat in the living room with Mrs. Annette. We talked and talked about everything. I fell in love with her wonderful, sweet personality. I asked her could I move into her house with her. She said, "If I did not have these boys, you could. I would love to have you for a daughter." The door opened and a tall, dark-skinned boy walked in. He said, "Who are you?" He was so handsome that I could not even speak. I ran to Mrs. Annette and I asked her who the little boy was. She smiled and she looked down at me and said, "That's my oldest son, Dewayne." He said, "Momma, who is she?" She told him, "She is Ms. Juanita's daughter." He replied in a deep voice that scared me when he talked. However, I still found him very attracted. I peeked out from behind Mrs. Annette, so I could not look up at him again. She just laughed at me. Dewayne walked up to me and said, "BOO!" I jumped farther behind her. She was still laughing at me. Dewayne walked upstairs to his room. A little girl came down the steps, and her eyes lit up. She said, "Momma you got someone for me to play with me." Mrs. Annette said, "Yes. You all can go outside and play. Go out the side door, and do not get out the garage." We went outside together. I looked across the streets, and there were some little boys playing basketball in the street. It was about six of them playing. Four of the boys were handsome. I heard them asking one of the little boys, "Who is that girl? She is cute." They stopped playing basketball and started staring at me. The side door opened up, and Dewayne came out of the house and walked into the garage where we were. He looked in the streets at the boys who were standing in the middle of the street looking into the garage. He asked, "What are y'all looking at?" All the boys started scrambling in the street acting as if they were playing basketball again. One of the boys said, "Just look at him showing out in front of that little girl!" I laughed at him. He turned around and said, "You all need to go in the house and read a book. The little girl, D, ran in the house. I rolled my eyes at him and said to myself, "I don't know who he is talking to." I sat on the bench. He said, "HELLO! I know you heard me." I just sat there, on that long bench that was under the carport, and laughed at him. I acted as if I did not hear him. He looked at me and said, "What are you laughing at?" I got scared then, but I just rolled my eyes and kept sitting on the bench. He turned his head and called Derek in the house. Derek started crying and came from across the street. Derek stopped and looked at me and said, "You are pretty." I blushed and said thank you. Dewayne said, "Derek get your pretty self into that house." Derek walked in the house. I was still sitting there. Dewayne walked up to me and grabbed me. I jumped. I was really scared then. He pulled me up from that bench and pulled me into the house. I started crying and broke loose from him. I ran to Mrs. Annette and told her to get her little boy because he was crazy. Both of them laughed together. Dewayne said, "I see that your tough self is in this house." I waited until he walked out the door, and then I said, "What's wrong with your son?" She smiled, with her beautiful smile, and said, "That's just his way of showing that he cares. He did not mean any harm. He was just trying to protect you. That's just his way of showing you that he cares about you." Derek heard Dewayne leave. He came down the stairs. He walked up to me and said, "Do you have a boyfriend?" I said, "No." Derek asked me to come up to his room so we could play. I told Mrs. Fisher that her little boy was trying to get me in his room. Derek said, "Momma I just wanted someone to play with." Mrs. Fisher said, "Derek go back up the stairs and play in your room." Derek ran up the stairs crying. Momma came down from upstairs and told Mrs. Annette that she had finished. Mrs. Annette asked Momma to give her a few minutes because she was waiting on Dewayne to come back to the house. She needed Dewayne to watch D and Derek. Dewayne walked in the house with a bad attitude, and went upstairs to his room. Mrs. Annette said, "Look at him; he's upset over his girlfriend." His deep, sexy voice howled from upstairs, "That's not my girlfriend!" We laughed at him and walked out the door. We went out the house and got into her car. We left her house and she took us home.

Momma and I walked in the front door of our house. She said, "I need to put this scrapbook together. Do you want to help me?" I asked, "What type of book is that?" She said, "It's my Closet Prayer's Book." I told her, "Sure, I want to help you. What do I need to do?" She said, "I need you to paste the prayers on a page." I asked, "All I have to do is glue it together? She replied, "Yes. That's all I need you to do." She pulled out two mid-sized boxes out of the closet. She passed me one the boxes, and she kept the other. I walked to the kitchen drawer and pulled out the brown Elmer's glue with the red plastic top. I saw the scissors lying on the counter top and picked them up too. I walked back to the living room and sat on the floor with Momma. Momma passed me a box that was packed with bible scriptures and some prayers that she had typed up. She had some brown, 8x10 thick, brown paper in a pack. She showed me a book that she had made by using brown paper, glue, and prayers that she typed. She had put it together and made it look like a photo album book without pictures. Instead of putting pictures in the book, we were putting in Bible verses and all kinds of scriptures in it. The cover page was named, Momma's Closet Prayers. I asked her, "Why didn't you call it Juanita's Prayer Book?" She replied, "That means that I would be taking the credit for God's work." I understood then, and I opened the first book up and began reading.

Matthew 6:6–8

6. *But thou, when thou prayest, enter into thy closet*, and when thou hast shut thy door, pray to thy Father which is in secret' and thy shall be rewarded thee openly. 7. But when ye pray, use not vain repetitions, as the heathen do: for they think

that they shall be heard for their much speaking. 8. Be not ye therefore like unto them; for your Father knoweth what things ye have need of, before ye ask him.

Matthew 6:30–34

30. Wherefore, if God so clothe the grass of the fields, which today is, and tomorrow is cast into the oven, shall he not much more clothe you. O ye of little faith? 31. Therefore take no thought, saying. What shall we eat? Or, Wherewithal shall we be clothed? 32. (For after these things do the Gentiles seek ;) for your heavenly Father knoweth that ye have need of all these things. 33. *But seek ye first the kingdom of* God, and his righteousness; *and all these things shall be added unto.* 34. Take therefore no thought for the morrow; for the morrow shall take thought for the things of itself. Sufficient unto the day is the evil thereof.

Right now, today, Lord Jesus I (put your name here) will trust you. I will seek your heaven. My eyes look toward the hills, which my help comes from the Lord. Amen. (Ps 123)

Matthew 7:7–8

7. Asked, and it shall be given you; seek and ye shall find; knock and it shall be opened unto you; 8. For everyone that

asketh receiveth; and he that seeketh findeth; and to him that knocketh it shall be opened.

One thing that God cannot do is lie. He is not like you or me. If His words say it, then He will do it.

7. Asked, and it (whatever is in your heart, ask Him right now) shall be given you; (Now its time to see in your mind, whatever you ask Him for. In addition, you have to believe it, is already done. Then give Him, his praise. Because He deserves it) seek and ye shall find; knock and it shall be opened unto you; 8. For everyone that asketh receiveth; and he that seeketh findeth; and to him that knocketh it shall be opened.

Luke 17:11–19

Suggested further reading: Psalm 130

How earnestly men can cry for help when they feel their need of it! (v. 13). It is difficult to conceive of any condition more thoroughly miserable than that of men afflicted with leprosy. They were cast out from society. They were cut off from all communion with their fellows. The lepers in this passage were aware of their wretchedness. They stood afar off but they did not stand idly by doing nothing. They felt acutely the deplorable state of their bodies. They found words to express their feelings. They cried earnestly for relief when a chance of relief appeared in sight. Their conduct throws much light on prayer.

How is it that many never pray at all? How is it that many are content to repeat a form of words but never pray with their hearts? How is it that dying men and women, with souls to be lost or saved, can know so little of real, hearty, businesslike prayer? The answer to these questions is short and simple. The bulk of mankind have no sense of sin. They do not feel their spiritual disease. They are not conscious that they are lost and guilty and hanging over the brink of hell. When a man finds out his soul's ailment he soon learns to pray. Like the lepers, he finds words to express his needs.

How is it that many true believers often pray so coldly? What is the reason that their prayers are so feeble, wandering and lukewarm? The answer once more is very plain. Their sense of need is not as deep as it ought to be. They are not truly alive to their own weakness and helplessness and so they do not cry fervently for mercy and grace. Let us remember these things.

Help meets men in the path of obedience (v. 14). Our Lord neither touched them nor prescribed means. Yet healing power accompanied the words he spoke. Relief met the afflicted company as soon as they obeyed his command. Surely this teaches us the wisdom of simple, childlike obedience to every word which comes from the mouth of Christ. It does not become us to stand still, reason and doubt when our Master's commands are plain and unmistakable (John 7:17).

For meditation: *'I need Thee every hour'*

5
IN NEED FOR COMPANY

Momma and I finished one more script book. She still had a quiet, few more prayers left. She had enough to make another book. My soul was at peace. My bottom was starting to heal.

Daddy came and picked me up. He wanted me to stay with him for a little while. We drove to Brush Allen. It was a town just before you got to Jacksonville. We drove up to a yard with many kids in it. All the kids looked just like me. Daddy introduced me to all of the kids in the yard, and then he took me into the house and introduced me to his brother, Golden, and his wife. I heard them talking about what happened to me. I heard Daddy say that he would kill him if he got out of jail. Uncle Golden said, "Do they have enough charges to stick it to him and keep him in jail.

Daddy said, "I hope not, because I want him to get out so I can kill him." Uncle Golden said, "Someone like him needs to be killed or locked up for life." I remember the little girl that looked like me. She tapped me on the shoulder and told me to come outside and play with her. She said, "I am your cousin Anita. We are getting ready to go skating. Do you want to go?" I replied yes. We went outside so we could play. I remember her brother staying isolated from everyone. I asked her what was wrong with him. She told me, that last week she shot their sister in the stomach and killed her. We went skating and had a good time. After the rink, daddy and I drove to Hot Springs, Arkansas where he lived. We drove up a long driveway, and we got out of the car. A woman, by the name of Faye, took me in her house. That is where I met Lisa, Regina, Little John and Shad. I was told that they where my sisters and brothers. Lisa said, "Momma I told you that I had a sister named Maria, and she is not your dead baby. I told you I was not crazy." I enjoyed not being the only child. The week was up and it was time to go back home.

The next day it was time to go back to the doctor for my following check up. The doctor said that my stitches, which he had put in, were healing well. They were still waiting on the rest of my tests to come back, and he still was not sure if I could have kids. Momma dropped her head with sadness in her eyes. I felt bad. I knew if I had listened to her in the first place, none of this would have happen to me. The more I looked at her, the more my consciousness started to play tricks on me. I could hear the devil forcefully telling me that this was my fault.

Summer was up and it was time to go back to school. The year of 1979, I was in the seventh grade. Momma had walked me to school so she could do my registration. We were in the front office, Momma had just filled out my paperwork, and she asked to see a counselor. The woman in the front called the counselor over so that I could meet her. She invited us in her office. We walked in, and Momma told her what had happened to me. The counselor was really a nice woman. She told me if I needed anything at all to let her know. We walked out, and a male student that was working in the office said, "Hello Maria." I looked at him to see if I knew him. Momma asked, "Is that your friend?" I said, "No, I haven't seen him before." As we walked out the front office, the counselor came out her office and told us goodbye again. Then she looked at the person that said hello and she said, "Reggie be a good boy, okay?" He said, "Okay Ms. Carol." We walked off to my classroom. I had another male teacher named Mr. Cheaterman. He was my homeroom teacher. He specialized in math. The next day I finally understood my crazy schedule, and I knew where all my classes were. The bell rang, and I was going up to the second floor to my third class of the day when I heard,

"Hello Maria." I turned around, and it was Reggie. He asked me if I had a boyfriend. I told him no. He wanted to know if I wanted to be his girlfriend. I put my head down and said "no" real softy. He got mad and said, "I didn't want you anyway, especially after you had 15 boys. I cried and said that was not true. He said, "I heard your Momma in the office telling the counselor that you were raped. Plus, I read the paper; I saw that you were raped by 15 boys." I started crying and some girl said, "Don't pay him any attention. He just thinks that he is all of that because he plays football." Another girl said, "You must have turned him down." I told her, in a soft, weary voice, that I did. They both said, "He is just Reggie, and he's like that. He is nothing but a big ol' baby. He thinks it is his way or no way at all." It still did not stop my tears from falling. All I could do was walk and think about how disappointed my Momma was when she looked at me. I thought about how I let her down. Weeks later, Reggie had the whole football team calling me "Big Fifteen." I was embarrassed, so I ran home. I said that I was not going back to school ever again. Momma walked me back to school the next day. I ran into Sherry in the bathroom. I told her about everything that was going on. She was going through a lot to. I told her I wish that I was dead, and she shared the mutual feeling. She said, "Let's kill ourselves." I said, "You are crazy." Sherry said, "Just think about it. Who would miss us?" I thought about it to myself. I knew Momma hated me, and plus, she worked all the time. Herman, my brother, did not know I even existed. Granny thought that I was the devil child because I was a raped. Sherry said, "Did you hear me talking to you? Wow! You were zoned out." I said, "Sherry, you are right. No one would miss me. Let's do this. She said, "Look in your Momma's medicine cabinet and bring all the pills you can find." After school, I went home and Momma was there. She said, "How was school?" I told her it was okay. I walked off and went to my room. I waited until she was asleep, and I went to the bathroom and looked unto the mirror where she kept all of her pills. All I could find was some Bayer aspirins. I grabbed them and put them into my book bag. I laid in the bed all night long trying to think of one reason why I should not take the pills. I heard Granny telling Momma, "That girl isn't good for anything. You need to teach her how to clean the house. She just won't be fit for nothing." The tears rolled out my eyes. I heard Momma reply to her, "Okay, calm down. I know, but I need you to relax yourself before you work yourself up into a heart attack. You just left the doctor, and he told you to try to relax more." That girl is going to be the death of me." The tears kept flowing until I cried myself to sleep.

The next morning, I ran to school and looked for Sherry. I found her and she told me that her problems were still increasing with her Momma at home. I said mines to. She wanted to know if I had brought the pills. I told her yes. We walked to the bathroom together. She had it all mapped out in her head on how to do it. She said, "I'll take a pill and drink some water from out the sink and you do the same with your pills. We divided the pills up in the bottle. We both had thirteen pills. By the time I got to the thirteenth pill, I passed out. I woke up to people standing over me, working on me. I was pissed off because all I wanted to do was die. I passed back out. I heard, "Do you know where you are?" I just stared into space. All I wanted to do is die. I went back out. "Maria! Maria! Get up baby. I love you. Get up!" I heard Momma voice, but I could not move any parts of my body. I heard her talking to God. "Please God! I do not understand why you have not made her respond. I give up Lord! I put it in your hands." My Momma was crying for the second time. I could not believe that she was crying over me. She was still talking to God for me. She was saying, "I don't understand God. Why do you have to take both of them at the same time? This is too much for me Lord. I can't handle this." She kept crying. I was trying to move but I just could not. I heard the nurse tell her to wait outside because I did not need to hear that conversation that she was having in the room with my body laying there in that condition. Momma told the nurse okay. The nurse walked over to me and rubbed my arm and side. She said, "You are going to be alright." The minute she said that, I was able to move my arms. She was still bent over me. She said, "I told you." She walked out and called the doctor. A team of them walked in my room and gathered around my bed. The doctor said, "I just gave you some charcoals and it's going to make you feel like your real sick. You gave us a real scare because we almost lost you." I never said a word. I thought to myself of not being with that praying Momma of mines. I started throwing up. The doctor walked back to me again and said, "See that's what I meant. You are going to wish you were dead by the time you get through throwing up." He laughed softly and walked out the room. Then he howled back in the door, "Come get me when she is done throwing up." I heard him outside the door talking to Momma. About 30 minutes later, he walked back in the room and said, "I am sorry for laughing at you. I did not know how much you had on your mind. Do you forgive me?" I nodded my head "yes," and I never said a word. Momma walked in the room. He turned around and told Momma to get me some counseling because I needed it. He wanted to know the counselor I had been talking to after I was raped. She told me that I did not want to go. He said, "She shouldn't have made that choice." Momma asked him, "Did she share any of her problems with you?" He said, "Well, no." Then she said, "Now why do you want me to waste my time and money? That's why I did not take to her to get any counseling." The doctor nodded his head and walked out the room. We went home and Momma cooked me some soup. She did not know how to cook, and Granny was getting sicker.

Momma went back to work. She was working many hours and running backwards and forwards to the hospital. I was at home most the time alone. I started trying to find my place in the world. I was sitting out on my porch and a woman that was two houses down was sitting on her front porch. She said, "Come here." I got up and walked down to her house. I walked to her and said, "Yes ma'am." She said, "My name is Traci and please do not call me ma'am." I sat down on the porch with her. I was bored to death. Traci said, "I go to school with you. I am in the ninth grade, and you are in the seventh grade right? I heard that you tried to kill yourself." I was embarrassed. I told her, "Yes, that was me." She told me that she worked part time with 911 as an operator. She said, "I was working the night that you were raped. I heard the call go through. Do you want to talk about it?" I said, "No." She told me that her door would always be open to me but some nights she had to work. She was taking care of her Momma, working, and going to school. I told her, "Thanks, but I am okay." Before she could get another word out, Sherry screamed in a loud voice, "Maria! What are you doing down there?" Traci said, "You are too nice to be friends with her." Sherry said, "Maria I know you heard me!" I froze and Traci said, "Go

What Goes On In Momma's Closet

ahead if that is what you want to do." I told Traci that I would see her at school. Sherry was walking toward me. Sherry looked at Traci and rolled her eyes. We walked off back toward my porch. Sherry said, "Where is your mean Grandma?" I said in the hospital. She said, "I hope that she gets some angry management classes." We laughed. Sherry said, "I never forgot about how she chased me at the house saying that I was the Devil Child." We laughed again. Sherry told me she wanted me to try something. She pulled out a pack of cigarettes. She gave me one and lit it up. I took a deep pull on it and started choking. She laughed at me. Before long, we both were laughing. I saw a taxi pull in front of the house, and I saw Momma in the back seat. Sherry grabbed the cigarette pack and took off running. I saw Momma look up as she was paying the cab driver. She got out the cab and walked to the front porch and I smelled like smoke. She said, "Are you smoking cigarettes now?" She was mad. Then she said, "I told you not to hang around that girl anymore. Does she have you smoking too?" I told her, "no." She looked very tired. She walked in the house, found some canned goods, and cooked it for Herman and I. Canned goods were the only thing that she could cook without burning up the house. She said, "Granny will be in the hospital for a while because she had to get a pacemaker put in to her heart. Granny's heart keeps skipping beats and the pacemaker would help her heart." While she was in the hospital, we were going to move to a bigger house. We ate and got in the bed.

The next morning I woke up to the crackling of crisp tape going across boxes. I popped up my head. Momma said, "Get up sleepy head. It is time to rise and shine. The movers will be here at anytime." I jumped up, went, and took a shower. While I was singing in the hot, warm bathtub, Herman said, "Don't use up all the hot water. Hurry up and get out of there! I need a shower." I jumped out the bathtub because Herman and I were not getting alone at all. I knew if I did not get out the bathtub, he would have beaten me up. I threw my clothes on, and I reminisced back to last week when Herman was playing with the BB gun in the house, and the BB pellets bounced off a wall and hit me in under my eye. It barely missed my eye by a half of an inch. I opened the door and walked out the bathroom. Momma laughed and said, "This is why we are moving. The next house has two bathrooms in it." I said, "I can't wait to move."

There was a knock on the door. Momma said, "I'll get it. The movers are early. They are not supposed to be here in to another hour." She opened up the door. She said, "What are you doing here? Do not come back to my house again. Don't you think you have done enough? Go away, and do not come back anymore. You are the evil child." Herman and I looked at each other and started laughing.

Then I heard Sherry's voice. In a loud tone she said, "As of Tuesday, October 1979, I don't want to come to your damn house anymore." Herman and I ran to the door to see. Momma reached towards her, jumped off the steps and laughed. Then, she took off. Momma closed the door. She turned and looked at me. She said, "You cannot play with that devil child anymore." Herman walked off smiling. He went to his room and finish packing his things. He had the biggest room in the house. His room had a large glass window on each side of his room. Herman called me into his room and showed me Sherry standing in the streets. He smiled and said, "Maria look at that your little friend. Aww! She misses you." Sherry was waving her arms in a motion telling me to come there. I heard Momma walking in to the room toward Herman and I. She said, "That evil girl was good for something." Herman asked her what it was. He had a big smile on his face. He was hoping Momma looked out the window and saw Sherry. Herman smiled and said, "Momma look out at the beautiful skies. It's so pretty outside." He looked at me and winked. I rolled my eyes at him. He burst out laughing. Momma caught on, and looked out the window, but Sherry saw Momma and hid. I glanced at Herman and smiled. Momma said, "I didn't know today was Tuesday. I thought that today was Wednesday. The movers do not come until tomorrow. I am working too many hours and doing too much. I am tired. I am going back to sleep and getting some rest. Maria do not get dirty because we are going to see Eleanor at the hospital." I said okay. She walked around the corner. I opened up the back sliding glass door in Herman's room and took off. I heard Herman call Momma and tell on me. Momma walked back to the door and said, "That little devil. I told her not to come over here anymore." Sherry and I walked to her house and sat on the back porch. We talked about her leaving me in the dark the night I was rape. The tears dropped from her eyes, and she said that she was sorry. I looked at her and told her that it was okay, but deep down in my soul I did not think she meant it. All she ever did was talk about Greg Williams. She would say all day how fine she thought he was. She lived in a fantasy world with Greg. I remember walking miles with her just to go by his house. Sherry said, "You are ashy. You need some lotion on." Then she said, "Let's go to A Day's Drug Store so we can get us some candy and lotion." I said, "I don't have any money." She said, "Awl girl, you don't need any money." We walked to the drug store that was behind her house. As we entered the store, she told me to ask the woman to show me where the lotions were. I did. By the time we made it back to the front of the store she had left out the store. There the little woman and I stood there in the front of the store. The woman rang up the lotion. She said, "That will be $1.90." I explained to her that I did not have any money and Sherry was gone. My eyes got big. My stomach was growling from lack of food. The woman asked me did Sherry put me up to asking for the lotion. I told her that she did. That woman grabbed my arm and told me to stop hanging around Sherry because she was not any good for me. I told her ok. She said, "If I catch her back in here I will call the police on her and if you don't want to go to jail then you better not be with her." She let go of my arm, and I ran out the store scared to death. I ran around the corner to go home. Sherry was sitting on the church steps laughing at me. I stopped and said, "That lady called the police on you." She said, "You believe that old bat?" I said, "Yes." She told me to sit down and relax my nerves. I asked her, "Why did you leave me in that store?" She said, "I was thinking about you. I knew you were hungry." Then she reached into her coat pockets and pulled out a hand full of Hershey's and Mr. Goodbars . She gave me half of her candy. We ate the candy and sat down on the church steps. I looked at the sign on the church which read Hoover Church. I looked at the street sign and it read West 13th. I looked back up the long, sidewalk that leads back to the drug store and I zoned out. While I zoned out, I was thinking about how Sherry was the reason for why I would get high. She told me to take it because it would help me forget about all the pain I was experiencing. I reflected on the flash party and the first house party that she took me to. She taught me a lot about how to live in the streets. Sherry had the street life figured out. She could have taught a class on Street Life 101. I knew that I had allowed her to influence me to do bad things. I also realized that I did not want to rot in someone's jail cell. As we walked back to her back porch and sat down, I told her that I was not going to jail and that I was sick of her with all her lies. I stood up on my feet. She looked up at me and asked me, "Where was I going?" I told her I was going home. I heard a doorbell coming from the inside of her house. I heard her Momma answer the door. I told Sherry that I was tired of running behind her. Before I could finish saying what I could say, her Momma walked to the back door. She said, "This is the second time your Momma has come over here. You know that you two are not supposed to be together." Sherry dropped her head and I walked to the front of her house to meet my Momma. Momma and Sherry's momma said goodbye to each other.

Momma started snapping about me hanging around Sherry and disrespecting her. I said in a soft voice, "I'm sick of Sherry, and I have no intentions of going back to her house." Momma kept fussing at me all the way home. One of the prayers I prayed the most was the need for comfort. I was so lonely. I had no friends, thanks to Sherry. She had run them all off.

A few weeks went by and Sherry popped up at my house. I was lonely. She told me about a party that they were having at Rick's Armonk. She said it was going to be all that. I took her word because she did know how to party, and she was familiar with where all the good parties were. Later that night, I snuck out the house. I got a new outfit and a new pair of booty pants. My black pair of Levi jeans fitted my little curves. The new pink shirt made my little boobs stick out more. I knew my outer appearance looked good, but my inner appearances looked ugly and felt bad. Deep on the inside, I knew that I was doing wrong. A part of me just wanted to turn around and go back home.

We walked all the way there. I was tired when we got there. I looked for a seat but there wasn't one. It was a lot people there, but I was not in a partying mood. Sherry pulled me on the floor. I danced for a quick minute, and then I walked off the floor. After two songs were over, she walked back to where I was standing. She asked me was I okay and I told her yes. But I actually wasn't ok. I just wanted to go home, but it was too dark for me to walk by myself. The Sugar Hill Gang was spinning smoothly on the turn tables, and it sounded good. I wanted to get my little groove on, but I didn't want to at the same time. Sherry was bouncing all over the floor. Another boy came and grabbed her hand. She looked at me and asked, "Are you sure that you are okay?" I said, "Yes gone and dance." She walked to the floor and stopped. Then she made a u-turn and walked back to where I was standing. She told me to gaze at the boy that was checking me out. I peeked over there and saw a fine guy. I popped my head back behind her. She laughed and walked back to the floor with her dance partner. The boy was so handsome. I wanted to look, but I was scared. I talked myself into it. I said to myself, "If I peek real quick maybe he won't know it." I caught my breath and looked over towards his direction real quick. He was gone. He wasn't in the same spot. I could not believe that he was gone that quick. How did I let him move without me knowing it? I turned my headed back to his direction where he once stood. Before I could turn back around someone tapped me on the shoulder. I gasped. It was him. It seemed like the loud music that once was playing just stopped. My heart started beating ninety miles per hour. I tried to act cool, so I slowly turned around. Before I could turn all the way around, I saw Sherry on the floor bent over laughing. I said to myself, "O My God!" This is not going to be good. I felt someone tap on my shoulders again. He said, "Hey I saw you checking out me. Were you just looking for me?" I said, "No.. No!" He smiled at me, and I went to wonderland by checking out every inch of his beautiful, Godly smile, and his sexy, long, slim body. I was speechless. He said, "What is wrong?" He got nervous. He thought that something was wrong with him. My stomach balled up in knots. I tried to tell him that he was fine. The words were caught up in my throat. He said in a nervous voice, "Let's dance." The words were still stuck in my throat. My body just followed him. That is all I could do. We danced on the floor all night long. I was in love with his tall, slim body. Our bodies fit perfect into each other as we danced to, "Play another Love Song." I gazed at his dark, flawless skin, his big, brown eyes, and his long, thick eyelashes. I loved his silky hair. He said, "I didn't think you wanted to dance with me." He told me that he was scared to ask me. I told him that I wanted to dance with him. He pushed me back gently, smiled, and said he was so happy. His smile made my whole world light up. I thought I saw fireworks. We danced to Teddy Pendergrass, and I fell in love. At the end of the night, Sherry interrupted Charles and I while we were on the floor. She said, "Hey we don't have a ride home." Charles said, "I will take you all home." Sherry said, "Okay." Sherry smiled at me and walked off. My heart started beating a hundred miles per hour. The light came on at the end of the party. We heard the DJ say, "You don't have to go home but you have to get out of here, so let's get to stepping! The party is over." Charles smiled and said, "Let's find your friend so we can get out of here!" He grabbed me by the hand and we walked off the dance floor to find Sherry. Sherry came up from behind us and said, "Hey love birds let's go." We both smiled and walked off to his car. About 20 cars later, we finally walked up to a two door, brown Sun Firer. It was two other guys there at his car waiting to go home. One of the guys said, "Hey man we all are not going to fit in that car. I told Charles that it was okay and that we will walk home. I turned to walk off and he grabbed me and said, "Hold on I have a solution. Sherry can sit in Robert's lap." Robert said, "That sounds like a plan to me." Sherry smiled and said, "Don't be trying any of that freaky stuff with me." He told her that she was not his type. We all piled up in the small car and went home.

Ms. Barbara called my house and asked Momma if I could babysit for her. Momma told her that I could start next week because we were moving into our new house tomorrow. The next day the movers came over and moved us into our new house on West 12th and Elm street. I started working for Ms. Barbra by babysitting her kids. I did not have a clue about babysitting. Her daughter, Pamela Rochelle, taught me everything that I needed to know. She also taught me how a real friend was supposed to be and act. I taught her about house parties. We started going to house parties together. Wc were having fun, but then we ran into Sherry. She had her famous funny cigarettes. Sherry passed it to me. I pulled on it and passed it back to Sherry. Rochelle asked, "What was that?" I told her to try it. She did. She took a deep pull on the cigarettes. She held the smoke in her mouth for while. Then she blew it out softy. We walked into the party. Rochelle said, "Look at that guy dancing in the corner." We looked. It was a man dancing so hard until he was sweating. Sweat was running down his face. It looked like he had just got out of the shower. He had on a loud, red colored suit. We were floating up so high until everything was funny. A guy behind me said, "That's Tyrone. "He just got out of prison." Sherry said, "We can tell with that ugly suit on." We laughed so hard at her because she could make the ugliest, sour faces. We laughed and laughed at everything that moved. That was the night I met Robert Challenger. He had given me his phone number. We talked for a long time at the party. I found out that he had just joined the Army. He explained to me that he would be leaving soon to go to basic training. After the party, we started walking home. A car pulled up. Robert wanted to know if we needed a ride. We jumped in his car, and he gave us a ride home. He had the prettiest, deep dimple that I had ever seen. He was tall and slim. He was not a bad looking man. He dropped everyone off before me. We stopped in the front of my house and talked for a minute. Then we went to the park and sat out for a while.

Everyday Robert came over to my house and picked me up. We were always going somewhere different. We went to Audio Creek where his uncle's house was. We walked to their door and I met his and uncle aunt. We sat in the den of their house. Then their daughter came from upstairs. She was gorgeous. He informed them that we were heading to the movies. His cousin wanted to go, so he told her to come on. She ran up the stairs and got dressed. After the movies, we took her home. The next day he picked me up and we went to Pizza Inn. We were sitting at the table enjoying the music, and he asked me if I loved him. I told him that I did. He informed that he felt the same way and he did not want to lose me. As the waiter walked up with our pizza, he asked me to marry him. The cheese and the scent of hot fresh bread aroma went up my nose. I could feel my stomach growling from the lack of food. The cute little waitress said, "Did you hear him?" I said, "No, I didn't." He smiled and repeated it again, "Maria I am getting ready to leave in a couple days, and I need to know if you really love me." He pulled out a beautiful, gold ring with a one-half karat diamond. He grabbed my ring hand, then he looked deep into my eyes. He said, "I am in love with you and if you really love me then prove it. Marry me." I gasped for breath. I replayed in my head how he had been treating me. He made me feel like I was a real woman. He was never disrespectful by staring at a pretty woman. He just made me feel like I was a gorgeous woman that he could not live without. I knew that I was number one in his life. He did a wonderful job taking care of me mentally and physically. I had whatever I wanted and needed. I was completely happy. The woman waiter said, "You put her into shock mode." They laughed and she said, "Honey we don't have all night to think about it." He got nervous and he asked me, "Are you sure that you love me?" I told him that I did. He let out a deep breath. I could tell he was relieved. He looked back into my eyes and I just smiled and said, "Yes, I will marry you." The waiter was relieved to. She shouted to the crowded pizza parlor, "Hello everyone could I have your attention for a small and brief moment?" It sounded like a million and one conversations stopped to listen. She continued and said, "These lovebirds right here are getting married." We smiled, and some of the people said congratulations. We smiled and he said, "Thanks." I heard some man say, "Someone is going to get lucky tonight." Then I was embarrassed. He reached and picked up a sliced of pizza that was on the pizza pan and put a piece on my plate. He watched me put my hands on the pizza. He stopped me and said, "This is how you eat a pizza. You need to cut the pizza up into pieces. You are going to be my wife and you need to learn how to be a lady." Some woman walked to our table and said, "Awl! That is so sweet. Congratulations you guys on your marriage. You all look like y'all are in love. God bless you all." He said, "Thank you." She walked off. Other people kept coming up to our table and saying the same thing. We ate and then we went back to my house. He walked in the door all excited and told my Momma and Granny that I said yes. They were happy about me getting a husband. Momma said, "Now you won't be in the streets as much." He said, "No I will not have that." Momma said, "Good." Momma and Granny went to their rooms and we went to mine. The next morning he had two days left before he was leaving. He told me that he was going to tell his family goodbye. He got up and disappeared out of the house. I was lying in the bed, and I heard someone knocking on the door. I got up and answered the door. Pam had a bright smile on. She said, "I saw your correction officer leave." She burst out laughing. I was a little upset about her making fun of me, but she was laughing so hard until I joined in with her. Then I realize how much I was missing her. We sat down on the front porch and Pam's eyes got big. She said, "Girl is he hitting you? I will beat his butt! He is just a little stick. I will break him in half!" I was ashamed. "No! He's not hitting me." She said, "Girl, whatever! Your face is purplish looking and it the size of his hands! Now I want to know what happen for him to do this to you. NOW TALK!" Tears started rolling out my eyes and I told her, "Please don't tell anyone." She said, "Is he hitting you?" I replied, "Yes." She asked, "Why? What makes him think that he is your daddy? His ass needs kids to beat!" I said, "He said that I was not lady enough and I needed to act with class because I would be carrying his name soon." Pam yelled, "What the hell! You are only fifteen years old. He needs to find a woman. Look Maria that is a nice ring but it is not worth your life. You are skinny, and it will not take much to break you in half. Get out of this relationship. He is too old for you. Just think about it. You will be changing his diapers soon." She laughed again, and I started crying. "Aw!! I am sorry but you need to get out of this before it is too late, okay? Hey walk with me to my house. I need to check in on my brothers." I said, "Okay. How did you know that I was by myself?" She said, "Girl I was sitting on the porch, and I saw his car. He pulled up to my house and spoke to me. I asked him where you were. He replied and pointed to your house. I was shock to see him without you. That is just not healthy with you two together all the time. You guys need some air and time to miss each other."

I was missing the time Pam and I used to spend together. Two hours later, Pam and I were still sitting on her porch. Pam asked, "Maria, why didn't he take you to meet his parents?" I said, "I am not sure. Pam replied, "He didn't think you were good enough to meet them." I got off the subject. She changed the subject, "Hey you remember being at the house party and Sherry was talking about the guy that just got out of prisons?" Pam burst out laughing. She stop laughing, "Don't look now but here comes your prison guard. Hey ask him why you can't meet his parents. Better yet I will ask him." I said, "No!" Robert said, "Hello Pam." She acknowledged him. "Maria you don't have to go with him." Robert said, "Hey let's go. I am hungry." I replied, "Okay I am coming." I was scared Pam was going to say the wrong thing and get him irritated. "Hey Maria, let's go."

Pam turned around real fast and looked at him. I jumped up off the porch, and I walked to his car. I refused to look back at her. I hollered at her, "I love you. See you later!" She never said a word to me.

He turned the radio off and he quickly glazed down my body. His eyes wondered back up to mines. "What do you have on?" I did not say a word. He slammed on his brakes. The car stopped! Our bodies bounced. He wanted an explanation to why my shorts were so short. I said, "I did not think about it. I was so happy to see Pam. We were caught up in our conservation to I.. I.. I just didn't think." "A wife does not wear things like that! Are you trying to catch someone else's eyes?" I said, "No, I am not!" He responded with an attitude, "I think you are lying. Is this the way you plan on dressing when I leave?" I said, "Robert it's not like I have a big choice on clothes." BAM! "You are lying! You should have put on a pair of pants." The tears rolled down my face. I told him that it was too hot to wear those pants. "I will buy you some clothes. I'll send you some soon as I get to my base." The swelling pains shot though my face as the tears kept running down. He said, "I am really sorry. It is just I get so angry at the thought of some other man touching you. I love you more than anything." He pulled my body closer to him. We drove off to get something to eat.

The next day the doorbell rang. I jumped out of bed, and looked down to see if he was still asleep. He was. I went to the door and opened it. Pam stood there and said, "I thought that you were coming back to my house." I smiled and walked out the door and sat on the front porch. I did not tell you that Pam. We both smiled. We were enjoying talking and I heard Robert at the door. We looked at each other. She whispered in a soft voice. "Now you know that he is crazy because he is too worried about what you are doing. Maria, what is wrong with your face? Did he hit you again?" The door opened up. My heart skipped several beats. Robert spoke in a kind gentle tone, "Hey Pam it's a little early huh?" She replied, "No its 2pm." He chuckled and shut the door. "Wow! Your guard is still standing at the door." Then in a low voice Pam said, "Girl that is a new bruise. That is not love. He has control issues. He is going to kill you. That man does not love you because love will not do that. Let me know when you want out, and I will be there for you." She shook her head, and she started walking out the gate. I yelled, "Pam, he does love me. I just need to act like I am his wife." She said, "Girl please, he is not your daddy."

Robert woke up the next morning. "I cannot believe I leave today. I am going to miss you baby." I responded, "Baby I will miss you too." He then grabbed my ring finger and stared at the ring he brought. He slowly looked up at me. He had tears in his eyes. "Maria, are you sure you want me? I love you with all my heart. I never meant to hurt you. I'll never do it again." He clutched my body close to his. He just held on to me. "Maria, I'm still waiting on your response." I said, "Robert I love you. You are my first boyfriend." He said, "I am not just a boyfriend. I am your companion, your soul mate. I will be your husband as soon as I get home."

I sat on the bed and watched him pack up all his belongings. Finally, he was through. We kissed and said our goodbyes. We walked out the side doors that lead to the streets where his car was parked. We hugged and kissed again. He climbed in the car, waved and drove off. I watched his car's tail lights disappear around the corner, I dropped my head. Part of me felt relieved, and the other part of me felt sad, hurt and completely alone. I was confused about the whole relationship thing.

6

CAUGHT IN THE MIDDLE OF A DEADLY HOUSE FIRE

A FEW WEEKS later, I ran into Ernest at the store. Ernest asked me if I wanted to go out with him. I said okay. He told me he would be by house at 7:00pm to pick me up. Two months later, I became very close to him. He asked me to be his girlfriend. I was excited about that. Ernest gave me a lot of attention, and I was not use to that, so I fell in head over hills for him. He was the perfect boyfriend. The only time he would put his hands on me was when he wanted to caress me. He would take me everywhere. I cannot count all the times that we went to the movies and out to eat. He was really spoiling me.

Ernest called me and told me we were going to attend a house party and that I needed to be ready around 8:00 pm. I told him that I wanted to spend some time with my girlfriends because she was back in town from Wrightsville. He told me to tell her she was going too. He always was good for showing up on time. At 8:00pm, he was there and ready to go. I was always the one that was running behind time. I came out about fifteen minutes later. I came out the house, and Rochelle and Ernest said at the same time, "It's about time you showed up." I laughed at them and tried to introduce them to each other. They told me that I was fifteen minutes top late on that. We all laughed and went to the party. Ernest was very excited about this party for some reason. We walked into the house, and I saw why he was excited. That party was all of that. It was packed with some good food and party people. It was the best party that I had ever been to.

We particd hard. Rochelle walked off the danced floor, came up to me, and said, "Oh my God! Maria, guess who just walked in this party?" Her eyes were big as if she saw a ghost. I got scared. I knew that Willie had just walked into the party, so I got my nerves up and asked her, "Who is it?" She was in a state of shock. She never said a word. I said, "Is it the man who raped me?" She told me that she did not know that man. She said, "Maria, hide over here because Robert just walked in!" I told her that I was going to hide. Then my little brain went into overload. I zoned off into memory lane. I remembered when Robert and I went out to eat at Pizza Hut and I picked up the pizza with my hands to eat the pizza. Robert said, "Why do you like to embarrass me like that? You do not eat pizza with your hand." Then he reached over the table and cut up my pizza with a knife and a fork. He looked at me hard and passed my plate back to me so I could eat it. He had that look in his eyes, and I knew when I got home he was going to make me call Jesus's name. Before I could finish my thoughts out Robert was standing in my face. He asked me, "What in the world are you doing at this party? I can't believe my woman is running the streets as if you do not have a man." He had that same wild look in his eyes like he had at Pizza Hut that night. Ernest walked up to me and asked me if I was ok. I was scared to death. Robert had a death grip on my arms. I told Ernest that I was fine. Ernest walked back to the dance floor and started dancing with Rochelle. Robert still had my arm in his hand. He looked me in the eyes and told me to wait a minute and I better not go anywhere until he got back. The song went off and he went around the corner. Rochelle and Ernest were walking off the dance floor laughing. Ernest asked, "Who was that?" I told him that he was an old boyfriend. He said, "He acted like a new boyfriend." He walked off to go get something to drink. I was terrified. I asked Rochelle if she could get Ernest to take her home because Robert had just threatened me. She said she would. I knew she would help me out because she was a true friend. She told me that I needed to face my fears and tell Robert to leave me alone, but I was too scared. She also expressed her concerns about riding home with my man. I told her that I trusted her. Ernest walked back up and gave me something to drink. I said, "Thanks" and took the drink.

I looked at Rochelle out the corner of my eyes and gave her a sign to get rid of Ernest. She was mad, but she did it. They left, and Robert walked back from around the corner. I thought to myself, "that was right on time."

He pulled me out the party. We got into his car and he slapped me across my face. He demanded to know why I was at that party. He told me that it was not lady-like to be at house parties, especially with me having a man. I mumbled, "Why were you at the party?" He smacked me again and asked me, "What did you say?" I did not say another word. I figured, if I just kept my mouth quiet, he would soon get tired of hitting me.

We finally made it to my house after that endless ride from hell. He came to my side of the car and pulled me out the car. He told me that he loved me and I should not have provoked him to hit me. We went into the house. All I remembered thinking about was Ernest, while he did what he needed to do. He rolled off me and held me as if he really loved me. We went to sleep.

I woke up to a knock on the door. He got up and answered the door. He walked back to my bedroom and told me to go to the door. I went to the door and Rochelle pulled me out the door and then she shut it hard. We walked out of my fence. She looked me in the eye and told me, "I knew I shouldn't have rode home with your boyfriend. He raped me." The tears rolled down her eyes. I felt so bad. I knew it was my fault. I told her that I was sorry. I heard the front door open. Then we saw him in the door. He called me back to the house. Rochelle told me to go back in the house before he hurt me again. I kept telling her that I was sorry. Robert started walking toward me and he asked, "What are you all talking about? Do not get quiet because I am out here. Rochelle, do not come back over here trying to set her up with some man. She already has a man." Rochelle ran off to her house. I started to go behind her. I felt so bad but before I could go. He had me in his arms holding me tight. I tried to get loose but he was too strong for me to fight. All I could do is tell her that I was sorry and the tears just flowed down my cheeks. I was so confused. Before I knew it, I was back in the house. He was sitting on top of me. He wanted to know why she pulled me way out to the streets. He asked, "Why couldn't she just say what she wanted by standing on the porch?" In his head, he knew she was trying to set me up with some boy. He told me that I should be glad to have a real man. I asked him did he think that he needed someone his own age. I could not believe I was only fifteen years old and I was with an eighteen-year-old man who was beating the holy crap out of me. Two weeks later, he decided to go visit his parent's house. This was the only place that I was not allowed to visit. He said it was because I did not know how to act in public. I was relieved that he had left me. Once he was gone, I had to debate with myself if I could go to Rochelle's house without him knowing that I was gone. Three hours later, I decided to go. I went over to Rochelle's house but her Momma said, "Rochelle is Wrightsville visiting her aunt." I asked her Momma was she okay. I told her to tell her that I missed her. I sat down on her front steps of her porch. My mind was running 100 miles per hour. I couldn't believe that I allowed myself to get my friend raped. I just could not believe that Ernest was that type of a man. I finally rose up my heavy body up off the porch. I walked back to my house. Just as I was going into the gate, I heard a car horn toot. I looked around the corner of my house and there was Ernest was getting out of his car. He said, "Hello you are a hard person to find. I have been sitting in the parking lot and that man would not let you go to the store." By the time he finished his statement, he was in my face. He took his finger and lifted up my face. He said, "Wow! Look at your pretty face. I can't believe that you allowed that man to do that to your face." I could see the pains in his eyes from the bruises on my face and the hickeys on my neck. He said, "That man don't let you go nowhere without him. How did you get away from him? I can't believe someone would hurt you like that." The tears from anger hurt and betrayal set in. I looked at him in his eyes and I said, "I can't believe you!" He said, "What?" I yelled, "I heard what you did to my best friend. You are no better than him. How could you do her or me like that? I love you…I really did care about you. Why did you do her like that?" The tears continued rolling down my face. He said, "Maria I was drunk. She came on to me and I am a man. I am sorry I did not mean to hurt you. I love you too." I said, "Ernest just go away." He dropped his head and slowly walked out the gate. He got into his car. Robert drove up. He parked his car towards Ernest's car. He drove off before Robert walked up to him. Robert stood in the middle of the streets and asked me who was he. I raised my shoulder up as to say I do not know. He walked into the gate on the fence. He said, "I just can't leave you anywhere. Why are you lying to me? I have eyes. I saw that man sitting in the parking lot across the streets the whole time." I knew it did not make sense to argue with a crazy man. The fight continued as we went into the house. Granny walked into the dining room where he was sitting on top of me. She said, "Robert you will have to get out of here with the fighting. I am too sick to be going through this." I wiggled to free myself. He looked up at Granny and said, "She is a wild animal and I am trying to tame her. At that point, Momma had walked into the house and said, "What is going on? I can hear you all way outside." Granny stood there with her cane and told him to get up off me." He turned around and addressed my Momma, "Ms. Juanita you told me to help you tame her. This is what I am going to do." Momma replied, "I didn't tell you to hurt her. While they were talking, I saw Granny's oxygen chain that held up her large oxygen tank up. I thought to myself, "I just need to wriggle over just a little bit more." I did it but he grabbed my hands and put my hands to together. Momma said, "Maria just mind him and he will stop. Now tell him you will do what it takes to be a good girlfriend. Then he will let you go." Granny said, "Let her go. You better be glad they stole my gun because I'll put a hole in your head." I wiggled my hand loose. I reached for the chain with one hand. He never saw it coming. It hit him in the back. I swung with all of my might. He fell over rolling on the floor. He screamed from the pains of the thick, strong, chain hitting him down on the floor. Momma told him, "I told you she was wild." I ran out the door. I took off down the streets. Twenty minutes later, I heard him driving down the streets looking for me. I ran back home and went in my door. Momma walk to my door and said, "That devil was pissing out blood. He needs to go to the hospital." I felt bad. A few hours later, I heard him walking through the house. It was too late he was in my bedroom. Momma laughed at him and walked out of my room. He said, "I need to go to the hospital come go with me." I said, "No." He grabbed me up off the bed and pulled me to his car. Momma and Granny told him to bring me back. He acted like he didn't hear them. He went and got a room in Jacksonville Hotel and we spent the night.

I went to bed praying that God removed him out my life. The next morning, he took me home. He used the phone to call into work. I could tell it was bad news. He hung up the phone and told me that he had orders to go to Germany. I tried not to look overexcited. That day, he walked out my life. Two or three months later he started sending me clothes from Germany.

7
CAUGHT IN THE MIDDLE OF A DEADLY FIRE

ROCHELLE FINALLY CAME back home and we learned how to skate together so we started going to the skating rink that was one block from my house. We would skate at the Giggle Skating Rink every Saturday night. Every weekend some someone was getting into a fight. The entertainment grew there and so did the crowd. The people would pack into the skating rink. You could barely walk through the aisle because it was packed with people from wall to wall. The skating floor would be crowded too. All you could here was people laughing and trying to talk over the loud music. Rochelle and I became close friends with, David, the owner. I started getting high and drinking with him. I became so close with him until we did not have to pay for our admissions anymore. That is where we met Jake the Snake. Jake used to be a preacher. He became our local free get high card. The drugs became my depression cure. It was my temporary heartache's relief. As long as I was high as a kite, I could find some of the stupid things to laugh about. It could give me the fast relief that I needed. I was able to bond closer to Jake the Snake. He listened to all of my problems and tried to find a solution for me. He taught Rochelle and me new things. He opened up our eyes to a completely new world. I looked forward to seeing him come to my house every day. One day, Jake told me he wanted to introduce me to his white girlfriend. I said okay. He pulled out a large freezer-sized bag out of his pocket. He told me to get him a hand-held size mirror. I did. He poured out the white powder on the mirror then he raked it into six even lines. He pulled out a hundred dollar bill and rolled it up like a cigarette. He held one side of the rolled hundred-dollar bill to his nose and he put the other side over the line of powder. Up went the line. It had disappeared up his nose. He smiled and said that it was refreshing. I thought to myself, "Hmm, refreshing. I want to feel refreshed." I told him I wanted to do that. He said then you need to go get a straw. I walked to the kitchen and found a straw. I took it back to the room. He took the razor blade that was on the mirror and cut the straw into half. Then he gave me one of the straws and told me to inhale the white line of powder up my nose. He held the straw while I inhaled deep. I rose up my head and told him that it burned. He told me to give it a minute. He told me that I needed to do the other side. I did. When I rose up, something felt different. I knew my body had sat up but at the same time I felt my little body had froze into place. All I could do is smile. I went over the moon and back again. I didn't have a care in the world. There I was, floating to planet X. I knew I was way out in the universe. I snapped out of my zone to him laughing. Back down on earth to his laughing. He said, "Are you okay?" I slowly said, "Yes, I am alright." I felt so light as if I could have flown away. The more Jake came over the more I wanted to meet his little, white girl. One day while we were in my bedroom I heard someone fighting on our sidewalk that was in the front of our house. He ran outside to break up the fight. He stopped the girls from fighting. They were still fussing but he stopped them from physically fighting. They were arguing over some boy who didn't want either one of them. The boy passed by them in some other girl's car waving at the girls who were just fighting on the sidewalk. The girls told each other that they were sorry and they walked off plotting together how to get even with the boy that they were fighting over. Jake said, "Well my work is done." We smiled and walked back towards the house. He said, "Let's go get something to eat."

At the time, Momma was working more hours and running back and forwards to the hospital with Granny. I hardly saw her. I remember Jake taking me to some high roller houses. I met a lot of people through him. We ate at a lot of fancy restaurants. I started gaining a few pounds. I was enjoying my new life. I remember him coming in the house with his pants stuffed with plenty of money. We would ride around town in his red and white Ford truck. I never forgot that truck. It was the first car that I learned how to drive in. We put many miles on that big, long, old Ford truck. After we went to Wendy's, we returned home. Momma was at the door crying, holding her cat in her arms. It was my favorite cat. I called her Smokey. She earned her name because every time we would smoke, the cat could smell it and come into the room. She would spin around in a circle and climb up the curtains. Jake said, "That cat was high." Momma was still in the front door upset with Jake and I because the cat sniffed his life away. I could not help but to cry as I stared at my kitty. She was stiff as a board. Momma told Jake, "I know you killed the cat with that stuff. Don't you come back over here." Jake told her, "Okay. But you have about ten more cats. If you don't want me to come back then I won't." A few months passed by and Jake soon disappeared. We hardly saw each other anymore.

The skating rink was slowly closing down because too many people were getting killed over there. Bowman Road skating rink was picking up Giggles skating rinks business. It was on the other side of town and I could not always catch a ride over there. I remember sitting on my front porch asking God for a ride so I could go skating. Rochelle and I's friendship started to die out. Her momma sent her back to her to Wrightsville to spend some time with her aunt because she was becoming too hot in the pants.

It was Saturday night and I could not find a ride to the skating rink on Bowman Road so I went to the Giggle Skating Rink around the corner from my house. That is where I met James McNealy. He was doing off duty security duties. He looked very nice in his sheriff uniform. I started talking to him and I was really enjoying his conversation. He was new to security guard duty at the skating rink. I asked him where was Uncle David. He said, "Who?" Then I explain to him that David Hart was the regular security person. I told him that Hart worked for Little Rock Police department. James told me that he knew who he was. James asked me if I had a boyfriend. I told him no. He gave me his number and told me if I needed anything to call him. I smiled and took his number. I stayed in the parking lot with James most of the night then I went home.

That following weekend I met Felicia Walker. She could get a ride anywhere. She was beautiful and bow-legged. I believe she used to be the best-dressed girl at Giggle Skating Rank. All of the boys were crazy about her. I loved her beautiful outgoing personality. She found us a ride to Bowman Road Skating Rank. Felicia and I became very close friends.

I remember waking up on Saturday morning and Felicia had brought me a pretty outfit by my house. She told me that she would be back around 7:00pm so we could go skating. She told me that the DJ from 102.3 radio station would be there so I needed to be ready. It was going to be the party of the year.

I looked at the clock and it was 7:30pm. I started to walk back in the house. I did not feel like going with female problems. I opened up the door and Felicia screamed out a car window that was pulling up. I jumped into the car and left with them. It was 11:00 pm and the lights came on. We were still partying. Then that night I met Brian Holiday. He was the DJ at the skating rank. He took Felicia out for breakfast and I caught a ride home with Roderick. Roderick took me out to eat. He asked me if I had a boyfriend I told him no. He said, "I am going to be your boyfriend." I said, "Ok." I walked in the house and fell deep into sleep. I heard, "Maria get up! The house is on fire!" My brother was known for playing tricks on people. I went back to sleep. I smelled smoke in the house. I heard the house cracking and popping. I opened up my eyes and saw smoke. I jumped up out the bed. Momma was coming back in to the house to get me. We ran out the house and went across the street.

The Channel 7 News was outside covering the story. The fire trucks started pulling up. Fire was coming out all of the windows and rising up to the roof. We barely made it out alive. Momma's cat caught on fire. We lost everything we had. Momma had so much stuff in the house. All her things gave the fire the energy it needed to spread faster. The house was totally gone. What the fire didn't destroy, the fireman did with their axes and water.

8
READY OR NOT, I AM MOMMA

THAT FALL OF 1982 we moved into the Holiday Inn hotel for a few weeks. We stayed until Momma got her insurance check. Momma worked at the Holiday Inn and we stayed there. Momma could not get rest because they always called her if they had an emergency. After two weeks, Momma and I rode around with Roderick to find a house to rent just until she received her insurance check. We found a house on 12th and Summit St, to rent. We moved there for a month. Roderick and I became close. No one told stories like Roderick could. He could make you laugh for hours. Herman, Roderick and I sat on the porch for hours laughing and talking about everything. I told them that I was hungry so I left them on the porch to talk.

I walked to the store. I crossed West 12th street and a police car pulled up to me. I thought to myself, "Why is this police officer messing with me?" I figured that if I did not look up, he would probably leave me alone. The car continued following me. I stopped and turned around to face the officer that was in the police car and all I saw was a big, pretty smile. I said to myself, "I know him from somewhere." I heard him saying, "Maria!" I was thinking, "I know this man just didn't call my name." I kept walking. He stopped the patrol car in front of me to block me from moving. I looked up and said, "James!" He started laughing at me. He said, "I was wondering when you were going to look up. Why haven't you called me?" I told him that my house burned up and I lost his number in the house fire. He said, "I knew that that was your house." He gave his number to me again. Then he drove off.

Later that day, I was sitting on the front porch and Jake popped up out of nowhere. I was glad to see him. He told me that he had better not see me talking to no police officer again. I asked him how he knew that. He told me that he had eyes everywhere. He drove off. I called James the next day; James came, picked me up and took me to his house. James was very entertaining but then he changed. I was not prepared for him to give me a lecture about school and life. I remember after eating at his house I started to feel tired and I fell asleep. I woke up the next morning and he was gone. I freaked out. My head was still spinning and I was confused about what had happen. I tried to line up my thoughts with my mind set but my mind was traveling at a fast pace. I stood up and I was dizzy. All I wanted to do was leave his house and go home. I walked to the front door and I could not open up the door. I walked back to the back of his house and found a back door but it would not open. I tried to open up both the doors in the house and I had no luck. I just could not believe that neither one of his doors would unlock. It was as if I was in jail. I sat down back on the couch and I felt so helpless. Then I looked around the room and saw a window. I walked to the window and it would not open. I tried to open up another window and I did not have any luck so I got a knife out of his kitchen and walked back to the window. I played with the window and it finally unlocked. I went back to his kitchen and put the knife back up. Then I climbed out the window and went home. That was an odd experience. I have never been at someone's house and could not get out.

A week later, Jake came and took me out to eat. He asked me all kind of question about James. I did not have any answer to give him. He looked confused. I was nervous because I knew him. He was good at taking people out for their last meal. I was so relieved that he took me back home instead of to the woods. I said to myself that I would never see James again.

I heard a horn toot outside so I walked to the window and peeked outside. All I saw was Roderick. I went outside to talk to Roderick. I told him it felt like something was missing in my life. I was tired of doing nothing every day. At that point, I finally decided to go school. I told Roderick that I have been out of school so long until I do not think that I could keep up with the work. Roderick said, "Maria as long as it is July 21st, 1983, I, Roderick Lane will tell you that you are going to do okay in school. Do you hear me?" I said, "Yes I hear you." I told him that I needed some school clothes. He said, "I will take care of it." I wanted to know when because he did not have a job. Momma came home and told us that she just closed on the house that was across the street. She had the keys in her hands. The house that we were renting was already half packed. Roderick, Herman, Momma and I moved everything in the house.

Granny got sicker so Roderick took her to the hospital. She told me that she was so tired and she wanted to go home. I said, "Granny, they are not going to let you go home." She told me, "Not that home Maria." I shook my head and thought to myself that she was crazy. A week later, she came home. She still was sick. She called me in her room and told me to get the banana out her drawer. I looked in the drawer and there was not any banana. I asked her if she wanted me to go to the store and get her some. She said, "No!" I started to walk out her room and she started talking to me. She asked me to get all those babies off the ceiling. She started counting all the babies she saw in her head. She said, "I can't take care of five babies. Do not have any more kids, Maria. That is too many mouths to feed. Father God, please take me home. That girl has too many kids." I said, "Granny, I don't have any kids." She went to sleep. I walked out of her room and climbed up in my bed.

The next morning, I woke up extra hungry. I went to the kitchen and there was no food. All I found was a small carton of milk. I drank it and it still did not satisfy my hunger pains. Momma was the only one who had money to buy some food and she still had a few hours to go before she could come home from work. I laid down in hopes to fall to sleep so I didn't have to think about not having food to eat.

I felt someone one shakes me. "Get up Maria. Did you drink my milk?" I replied, "Yes Herman. I was hungry." He said, "What? I cannot believe you drank the milk up. Maria that milk was mine." I sat up in the bed. I saw Herman's feet go up in the air. Then I felt myself flying off the bed. Blood was everywhere. Herman's foot went hard against my mouth. The hungry pains were gone but the pain that I had in my mouth was very real. I got up off the floor and ran to the bathroom. I looked in the bathroom mirror at my mouth. My mouth was cover in blood and I had a deep spilt in my mouth. Granny walked and knocked on the bathroom door. She told me to open up the door. I did. She said, "O my God. Boy why did you do your sister like that?" She called Momma and told her to come home so she could take me to the doctor. All I could do is cry. I was in so much pain. Before Momma could come home I had used up two bathroom towels. I was trying to stop the bleeding. I kept trying to tell Granny thank you for getting up at to take care of me. She did not hear me because she was still fusing at Herman calling him the devil child. I heard the front door open. Momma ran up to me grab my mouth and looked in it and blood was still coming out at a rapid pace. She screamed out at Herman, "First you tried to put her eye out with a BB gun and now you have split her lip. You better be gone when I get back from the doctor." We got into the taxicab that was parked in our driveway waiting on us. We headed to the doctor's office.

The doctor checked my mouth and he told Momma that I did not need stitches and that the mouth was one part of the body that recovered the fastest. He asked me when the last time that I had a period. I really could not remember. I told him I thought that I had it about a month ago. He said, "You should keep up with your periods. Are you sexually active?" I replied, "Yes, I am. "He said, "Then a busted up mouth is your least concerns. You need to be worried about being pregnant." Then he ordered the nurse to do a pregnancy test on me. Momma said, "What? Girl you better not be pregnant. I cannot take care of a baby. Do you think that I am working hard enough?" While she was fussing, I was thinking to myself, "Woman I am not pregnant." The doctor walked back in the room. He came up to me, looked me in the eye, and said, "What would you do if I told you that you are pregnant?" I said that I am not worried about that because I am not pregnant. He said, "Guess again, because you are pregnant. You are going to be a mother. You are only 17th years old. Next at this time you will be a mother. You do have others options, because there's a lot of women that can't have kids. This baby can be a blessing to someone else" Then he addressed Momma and asked her, "What are you going to do about the fellow that kicked her in the mouth? Was that her baby daddy? You need to file charges against him because he could have made her lose her baby." Momma was in total shock. She could not move or speak. The doctor had his back toward her and he noticed that she was not responding to any of his questions. He turned around towards her and looked at her. I believe his heart went out to her. He said, "You really had no idea, that she could have been pregnant did you?" Momma shook her head no. Dr. King said, "I understand that you are in shock mode. If it were I, I would be to. You clothed them and feed them and you try to raise your kids to the best ability, as you know how and it is still not good enough." Momma said, "We can't afford another mouth to feed right now." Doctor King said, "Now there are other options, like an abortion or adoption. Now I am not a baby doctor so if you plan to keep this baby you will have to find a pediatrician." Dr. King walked out the room. Momma talked to the nurse and got a few prescriptions. Then she called a cab. The cab dropped us off at the drug store. Mr. Daniels, the pharmacist, filled all of my medications and then we walked home.

Finally, I was back in my room. My mouth was still in pain. My life was moving fast. I heard a knock on the door. I told them to come in. Granny said, "I told you that I saw your babies on the ceiling. Lord, take me home. I am ready to go. I can't take care of all of those babies." She walked back to her room. That night, Roderick came over and I told him that I was pregnant. He was happy about being a father.

August was finally here and it was time to go back to school. My morning sickness was coming too. I was late to my first period class everyday because I could not stay out the bathroom. Seven weeks of school had gone by and it was time to get my progress report. I had a good feeling that my grades were good. I walked in to my homeroom teacher Ms. Paxton. She said, "You are on time. I can't believe it." She had everyone's progress reports in her hand. She started passing them out. She gave mine last. She looked at me and said, "Just because you have good grades don't mean I won't flunk you because attending class is just as important as your grades." She walked off and I rolled my eyes. She started class. I remember jumping up because I had to go to the bathroom. She said, "Stop!" I turned around and looked at her. She wanted to know where I was going in such a hurry. I told her that I needed to go to the bathroom. She said, "Don't go on my clock. If you walk out that door, don't come back." I said okay. I walked to the bathroom. Then I went jumped in my 5.0 GT and headed home. I pulled up to the house and the ambulance was parked on the side of the house with their lights on. I saw the front door open. I walked into the house and there was Granny stretched out on the stretcher with an oxygen mask on. The men were working on her. I could not do anything but cry. My Granny was deteriorating right in front of me. This same woman could shoot a snake out of a tree from a block away. Now she did not even have the strength to be on her own. I felt so helpless. My Granny was dying. They took her to the hospital.

Granny was still hanging on to life. She wanted to see her first grand baby. I was thirty- two weeks along the way. We were happy that she was beating the odds. She had already beat the dead line that the doctor had giving her. She was headed back home from the hospital. I had her room clean and ready for her. Granny came home right on schedule. I fixed her some chicken noodle soup and gave her a banana on the side with a glass of water. I sat down and watched her eat her food. She turned around and said, "I am tired. I am too weak to hang on. I am not going to be able to see your baby." She rolled over and went to sleep. I sat in the chair feeling helpless. I just sat there and tears rolled out my eyes. I sat there trying to reason all those thoughts that were racing in my head. I kept staring at the rain that was falling fast as fast as the tears that was coming in my eyes.

A week later, Granny gave up her fight, March 2, 1984. She finally went home to our Father. A few days later, I woke up with strong pains and pains in my bottom. I went to the hospital only to be sent back home because I was having a false labor.

The next day I headed back to the doctor because I was 32 weeks. I had gained sixty -two pounds. I went from a size zero to a size ten. I was so big until I could not see my feet. The doctor told me that my baby should be here another week because I had dilated two centimeters. One week later, I woke and started cleaning the house. I wanted some greens. I went in the kitchen to put some on and I felt myself urinating. A small sticky line of junk ran down my legs. I called Roderick and told him to come get me. The pain was so intense until my screaming woke up Herman. He jumped up and told me to stop screaming. I said, "But.. But, I am in so much pain." The trail of tears told him that

I was in trouble. He jumped right into action. He helped me get into the car. We took off in the little Mustang and headed to the hospital. I think Herman found all the bumps in the streets. He only found the bumps in the road when I was having contractions. At the same time, he was fussing and cursing because I woke him up. Then, he told me not to have that baby in his car. He fussed at me all the way there and I screamed in pain all the way there. We finally made it to the hospital. Herman was more nervous than I was. I told him that I was the one having the baby not him. He ran in the hospital and got a wheelchair and came out to get me. He still managed to find every bump while he was pushing up the ramp. They told him to take me to labor and deliveries. I was powerless and the pain was out of control. It felt like I was dying. They said death go over you nine times. They underestimated that statement. I wanted to die. The pain was in full control of my body and I sat helpless at the mercy of anybody. My contraction was every ten to fifteen minutes. All I could do was sit in that wheelchair and wait on Herman to get me in to see the doctor. My stomach tightened up real tight. Herman pushed the wheelchair up to the door of the labor and deliverer and he realized that he had to push the button on the wall to open up the door. He pushed the door button on the wall but he forgot that I was in front of the door. The pain had just eased up some. Then I felt myself flying backward down the hallway. Herman said. "Oops!" Then he ran down the hall to catch the chair. Herman grabbed the wheelchair and said, "Maria you are going the wrong way. Look like you forgot about your pains for a minute." He laughed and pushed me through the door. The nurse took me from him and helped me get into the bed. Thirty-six hours later, I had a seven pounds and fourteen ounces, baby girl.

Three years later, it was 1987. I found myself in New Baptist Medical Center and I was on my third child. She was seven pounds and eleven ounce. The love of my life was not even there. I found myself alone again having his baby. There I was alone giving birth to his child. I cried myself to sleep that night. Momma, my one true friend, came to the hospital the next morning to pick my baby and me up. Momma was always there for me and I always was too blind to see it. Momma had my house clean and spotless. Shirley had a hot meal on the table for me. All I could do was think about my baby daddy so I drove off with my baby. My brother and my Momma would not let me go by myself. We pulled up to his momma's house where he was staying. I took my baby in his momma's house so they could see my baby. While they were enjoying my baby, I pulled George off to the side. I wanted to know why he was not there with me while I was giving birth to his baby. He told me that his momma told him that she had seen a big black man in my door and that the baby was not his. I was shocked. I grabbed my newborn baby and told my other two kids to come along and we left out the house. I was mad as hell. I jumped in the car with my Momma, brother, and left.

Three weeks later, I found myself raising three kids and a grown child. One week later, I was tired from running behind all the kids in the house and all I wanted to do was sleep. I heard my mother come into the house. She walked in my room with Crystal Gale (my last baby) in her arms. She said, "Get up! Something is wrong with your baby." I said, "Okay Mother" and I rolled back on my side and went into a deep sleep. Thirty minutes later, my phone rang. I was mad as hell. I could not sleep. No one would get the phone. I jumped up and George was on the couch. He was into a game and the kids were outside playing. I picked up the phone and said, "What?" Momma's voice was on the other end. She said, "Get here now!" I was confused but I knew that tone in her voice was not right. She said, "Its Crystal! They just called code blue. She is dying! Hurry up. She will probably be dead by the time you get here!" I screamed. George jumped off the couch. He wanted to know what was wrong. I told him that we had to go, that Crystal was in the hospital, and they had called code blue.

Six months had gone by and I was spending most of my time in the hospital between my other two kids. I was going crazy. I was walking on eggshells. Every other week if I was at the hospital they were calling me back to the hospital because they were calling code blue on my baby. Then I heard about a hospital in Lana Linda, California. They specialized in babies with heart problems like Crystal. I called the hospital and talked to a nurse on the phone so I could ask about the programs. She wanted me to give her Crystal's history so I did. I told her, "My baby girl was born on April 24th. She weighed 7lbs and 11 ounces. One month later after I had her, she had a heart attack. She had a valve that grew backwards. That caused her heart to work harder and strain. I have been back and forth to the hospital and I am tired. I want to know if I need to get on the transplant waiting list." The nurse explained to me that she could not make any promises. However, she suggested that I needed to bring Crystal there so Dr. Bailey could see her. She gave me all the information that I needed. Momma helped me raise money for Crystal by going to the local newspaper and television stations. It did not take long at all to raise the money so Crystal and I could go to California.

I asked George if he could go with me but he found every excuse in the world for why he could not go. Crystal and I headed to the airport. By the time, we go to the airport, the local newspaper and television station met us there. I gave them a progress interview before we boarded the plane. Crystal and I got on the plane and headed to California. Crystal went through all kinds of tests that week. They could not find her vein to stick her IV needle in. I could not stand to watch her cry anymore so I went to the hotel that I was staying in. I remembered looking at the clock, it was around 9:30 pm, and I rolled over to go to sleep. Then I heard someone rattle the door. The sound was coming from the door next to my room. I got quiet to see if I was hearing things. Then the rattling noise was back. Someone from the room that was on the side of my room was trying to come in the joining room door. I freaked out. I thought to myself, "I am going to die in this room and I will not get a chance to tell my mother and kids goodbye." Then the phone rang in my hotel room. I jumped up and got the phone. It was my mother. I cried and told her someone in the next room was trying to come in. The rattling started again. She said, "Call the police right now!" I hung up phone, called the front desk, and told them to call the police because someone was trying to come in my room. The man said, "Ma'am I am standing in the front of the hotel and I don't see anyone." I informed him that the person was still rattling my door from the inside. Then the noise stopped. I hung up the phone. My phone rang again. It was my mother. She told me that she going to catch a flight out her so she could be with Crystal and me. We said our goodbyes and we got off the phone.

The next day mother came to California. We sat at the hospital all day with Crystal. Crystal enjoyed all the attention we were giving her. Few days later, I finally met Dr. Bailey. He was known all over the world for being the best doctor in the world for being able to perform a heart transplant. It was an honor to meet the man who could possibly save my daughter's life. Here I stood shaking Dr. Bailey's hand. I was excited about this. I never understood why people got so excited about meeting celebrities. I only felt like that, because most of those only get rich off of us. They would see us in person and would even want to have anything to do with you. All they want is for you to do something for them. They want you to watch their shows so they could get ratings or they would endorse something so they could make a profit. Doctor Bailey was my celebrity. He had the power to give comfort to a suffering person. He really made a difference in many family's lives. He was very underrated and underpaid. There I stood face to face with the famous Dr. Bailey. I was happy. Dr. Bailey told me that to put Crystal on a transplant list would be a waste of time. My heart sank in my chest. I was hurt. I never felt so alone. The tears rolled down my face. I asked him why. He explained that Crystal only had two weeks to live. I just knew I was going to faint. He sat down with me. Then he asked me, "Do you like to see her in pain?" I said, "No." He said, "Your baby is living a bad nightmare. It is amazing she is still here. I do understand. Her little body is too deteriorated for her to get on a waiting list. If you truly love her, let her go. She is in too much pain." I could not hold my cries back anymore. I knew he was right but at the same time, my selfless love wanted to hold on to her. He grabbed me and hugged me. Then he said, "I am sorry. If I open up her body, she will die. She would never make it out of surgery. I am sorry. Have a good day." I met with the board of the hospital later on that day. After the meeting, a black man walked up to me and he introduced himself to my mother and me. He said, "Hello, my name is Dan and I am the head of Public Relations. I deal with the media and other public relations. Do you want to talk to the press?" I told him no. He wanted to know what I planned to do. I informed him that I wasn't sure. He invited me to stay in California. I told him that I couldn't afford to stay. He also told me that he could set me up with a place to stay and he could arrange for me to get a job there in the hospital. I explained to him that I had other kids in Arkansas. Mother butted in on the conversation and said, "That's crazy. She doesn't have family or friends here. Plus someone just tried to come into her room." He said, "What?" He took all of my information down about where I was staying. Then he told me that he would see to it that I was taken care of. I sat back and thought about it. Then George ran across my mind. I knew I was still in love with him. Then I told the man no. He gave me his business card with his personal cell number on it. He told me if I changed my mind, he could arrange to move me and my kids back to California with no questions asked. He did not understand how I could want to stay in Arkansas, which was "the land of no opportunities for coloreds." He said, "I will have my jet to fly you back home. I need to set up a team of doctors and nurses to accompany you back home. Okay?" I said, "Okay." I had never met a black man with that much power. That was truly amazing. I was just overwhelmed about everything that was going on. I called my sister and told her what was going on. Lisa was staying in my house at the time so I asked to tell George to pick me up from the airport tomorrow.

The next morning, he did just what he said he would not do. We all boarded the private jet and headed to Little Rock. We went through a storm and the lightening was coming through the jet windows. I turned around and asked the Cardio Doctor to come check my heart because the lightening went to the window and scared the life out of me. I think everyone was a little nervous. Three hours later, we were landing. I called my house and no one answered the phone. Mother and I walked home from the hospital in the rain. I was grateful that we only stayed five blocks away. Mother and I stayed across the street from each other. She went to her house and I walked into my house. I was soaking wet. I was pulling my shoes off by the door then I heard people laughing. I said to myself, "I know that I don't hear anyone laughing up in my house."

I know no one was sitting in my house having a good time while I was struggling with suitcases and walking in the rain. I heard them laugh again so I walked to the bedroom and stood there. Then George looked up at me and said, "Uh-oh!" Lisa said, "I forgot about you. Sorry!" I said, "What the mess? I can't believe this. Four people are just sitting my house, on my bed playing a freaking board game!" I was so angry. I was pissed off. I said, "All of you have cars and no one even bothered to come pick me up? I have been through hell and back again! I had to walk home with two big suitcases." Chris Matthews jumped up and said, "Well that's a sign, I guess the game is over." I said, "It sure is." Everyone else jumped up too. I was so mad to the point that I did not even care who left out of my house. Lisa grabbed the board game and said, "I guess we can all go up to Francis May's house." George said, "Well let's go." I told him, "Go, I don't care. That is what you do best. You are always running. Go to your mother's house little boy." Then they all left my house. I continued taking off my wet clothes.

It has been over two weeks since I was able to lie down in a bathtub. I went and soaked in the tub and thought to myself. Right now, California is starting to sound good. I couldn't believe that Lisa and George both let me walk home in the rain. Neither one of them did not even care enough to go see my sick baby. I just told them over the phone that she had less than two weeks to live. It was okay that they did care about me. I was completely confused. Lisa was Crystal's aunt and George was Crystal's father. None of them even asked anything about her or about her condition. Once I got out the tub, I wrapped up in a towel and went to my purse and I pulled out the card with the man's name on it and dialed the number. The number went straight to voicemail. I hung up the phone and I was lost for words. I said to myself that I would call him tomorrow. The next day came and I was at the hospital with Crystal. George walked in Crystal's room and I walked out. I wanted to give him some time with her. He walked out behind me. He grabbed me and told me he was sorry. He asked me to sit in the room with him. I walked back in the room with him. Crystal started talking to her daddy. It melted his heart. Then he realized that he loved her and he was doing everything to prove it. George and I were going backwards and forwards in our relationship. Meanwhile, we sat in Crystal's room watched the television, and caught the five o'clock news. It caught my attention. I said, "Hey, George that is the motel I stayed in when we were in California. Oh my God. They found a serial killer there. I told you all that someone was trying to get in my room. I call the motel office clerk and he said no one was next door to me. I know I was not crazy. That man was going to try to kill me. I know it. They told me I was crazy."

I was sick and tired of fighting. I wanted off this emotional rollercoaster. One week later, George and I were in Crystal Gale's room and we decided to go and get something to drink. On our way we back, we saw people crowded in her room. We walked in and they said that they were sorry. I said, "What is wrong?" No one said a word. They all had tears in their eyes. Everyone that worked at Arkansas Children's Hospital knew Crystal and everyone fell in love with her. Her room was crowded. People started walking out of the room. I looked at the bed and my baby laid their lifeless. My whole world had just passed me by. I could not believe that that was the last time I would see my baby. George just grabbed her out of the bed and held her lifeless body. He held her for a few minutes. I thought that I had experience a lot but nothing could prepare me for this. My heart felt so dead and at the same time, I still could not believe that she was gone. The media team was outside the room trying to get an interview and I was in no shape to talk to them. The doctor walked in the room and told me it was time to take Crystal's body.

I woke up the next morning and my eyes were still heavy from the tears that I had cried. I cried myself to sleep. I was hoping that I had just had a bad dream. Mother walked in my house and she had the newspaper in her hands. She read the newspaper article, "Baby Crystal Gale, born on April 24th gave up her fight January 2nd." I looked at the newspaper and she was on the front page. I turned on the television and she was on every station. I knew that I wasn't dreaming. My daughter gave up her fight.

George and I's relationship was not getting any better. One day he loves me unconditionally and the next day could not stand me. He was the first man that loved me and I loved him back. How did I get myself into this? I do not understand how our relationship got to this point. George walked in the door and interrupted my thoughts. Now I am just pissed off. All I wanted was for him to get out the house and gone so I put him out. Few days passed by and I was sick as a dog. I went to the doctor just to find out that I was pregnant again. I did not want to tell him that I was carrying his child. I know the first that his mother was going to say. I hear her saying, "She knew what she was doing. She was just trying to trap you." I promised to myself that I would never date a mother's baby anymore. I heard a knock on the door. It was George. He looked so sad. My heart went out to him again. I loved this man so much. He wanted me back I was so evil to him. He did not care. That was why I loved him so much. Regardless, what had or did happened, he stood by my side. I took him back. I was in love all over again. I told him that I was carrying his baby. He was happy. I told him that I did not want to go through any more drama with him or his mother. He said, "We need to move to a new state so we can start over."

I agreed to go with him to Washington. I sold everything in my house so we could start our new life. After the yard sale, I was having some pains. I went to the bathroom and sat on the toilet. The pains were so great until I could not move. I felt something warm coming out of me and the pains eased up. I stood up and looked down and there was my little baby lying in the toilet. He was still in his bag. I called George and Herman in to see my baby. I guess from moving all the furniture had made me have a miscarriage. I cried myself to sleep. The next morning, I was in a better mood. All I could do was think about me and George moving to Washington. I heard George come in the house. He did not look like his normal self. I asked him what was wrong. That was a big mistake. He decided not to move to Washington. I wanted to know why. He did not want to tell me. I asked him where was he coming from and he told said he came from his moms house. I got pissed off. I said, "You were moving to Washington before you left out that door and now you go to your mother's house and you just happen to not want to go? I mean I just sold all of my stuff." Enough was enough. I put his sorry, broke butt out of my house and broke up with him. I had had enough and I was fed up with him and living my life to please his family.

Few months went by and I was sitting on my front porch. A car stopped in front of my house. I looked into the car and I saw a sexy man in the car. He asked if he could get out and talk to me. All I could do was nod my head. He got out and stood up. My mouth dropped open. This man stood about six foot two and he had a slim, toned body. His flawless, smooth skin was a caramel color. He noticed that I was checking him out. He smiled and all I could see was his beautiful smile. This man had the face and body that every woman dreamed of. He said, "Hello, my name is Andre." I told him my name. Then I told him that I saw him from somewhere before. I knew that was first time that I had seen him. I was just trying to figure out where he worked at. He was too fine to be a total package. He said, "I work at the Little Rock Fire Department." I said, "Wow!" He really was a total package. He asked if I would like to go out with him sometimes. I told him that I would. We started talking on the phone often. I was growing close to Andre. I was just at a happy point with him. Then George started showing back up.

I told myself that I was strong enough to deal with him only on a friendship basis. I only found out that I was lying to myself. I stopped dealing with Andre and went back to George. Few months later, I was pregnant again. Months went by and I found out George had cheated on me again. I hated myself for being foolish when it came to him. I remembered wishing that I had never carried his baby. A few more months had gone by and I was in the hospital having his baby again. I told the nurse that I could not believe that I was having another baby again. Momma said, "Ready? You are a mother!"

I tried to give up the fight about being in a relationship with George but I was not having any luck with the fight with myself. One day he wanted to marry me and the next day he did not. Lisa and I made up and I worked hard at building a relationship with my sister. They say, "Blood is thicker than water. "I was telling Lisa about how George and I talked about getting married. Then she informed me that George was seeing another woman named Margie. Then, she broke the news to me gently about him marrying someone else. She gave me all of us Margie's and the other woman's information. I decided to go to by Margie's house to see if he was cheating on me. I waited for him to leave the house. I gave him about an hour before I left the house. I put the kids in the car and went by her house. I pulled into the apartment where she stayed. I went around the corner and saw George's car sitting in the car parking lot. I pulled up beside it and sat there for a few minutes. I had all these wonderful thoughts in my head on what I would do. As soon as I saw his car, those thoughts just dropped out of my head. I looked for a brick in the parking lot but I did not see one. I drove back to his car and I wrote a note to him and told him not to come back to my house ever again and that whatever he had at my house, I was going to burn it.

I was madder at myself than being mad at him. I could not believe that I was carrying his child and he was trying to get some other woman to marry him. I resorted back to the books mother had put together. It was time to return to God. Mother's prayer closet books had pulled me through many things. The first prayer that was in the book was…

9
CAUGHT IN THE MIDDLE OF A DEADLY BATTLEFIELD

Father God, I ask for grace to trust you more. When I am afraid, I will trust in you. I praise your word, my Father God, in you I will trust; I will not be afraid. What can mortal man do to me?

Therefore, I am not anxious [beforehand] how I shall reply in defense or what I am to say, for the Holy Spirit will teach me in that very hour and moment what [I] ought to say to those in the outside world. My speech is seasoned with salt. Thank you Father God…Amen.

Father God, I believe that you have heard my groaning, my cries. I will live to see your promises of deliverance fulfilled in my life. You (Father God) have not forgotten one word of your promise; you are a Covenant-Keeper. It is You Who will bring me out from under the yoke of bondage and free me from being a slave to _____. You (Father God) have redeemed me with an outstretched arm and mighty act of judgment. You (Father God) have taken me as your own, and you are my God. You are a father to me. You are my God; you are a father to me. You have delivered me from (_____) and I just want to tell you thank you, Father God. Amen.

I could not believe it was 1991. My life had just passed me by. I was a mother of three living kids and I did not have a clue on life or what to do with my life. I wished life had given me written directions or manual on what to do with a screwed up life. I was drugging and drinking. I was partying all the time. Wherever I went, I always had the devil in my cup, as my granny called it.

I walked out and sat on my porch. I was just sitting on my porch while the kids played in the yard. Then a man stopped in the front of my house. He asked if he could come up and have a seat. He was hot and wanted a cup of water. I went in the house and got a cold glass of water. Then he asked if he could have a plate of whatever that wonder aroma was coming out of the kitchen. He asked me what was wrong with me. I told him that I hate people. He laughed at me. Then he said. "I understand that feeling towards folks. However, it takes all kinds of individuals to make the world work.

What Goes On In Momma's Closet

God created every human being with a certain purpose her in His world to do His will. We might not agree with His plan but I will promise you one thing. It will work out for the best in the end. In order to move forward to the future, you have to leave the past behind. You have to let go in order to let God do His thing. You have to want to stop suffering, in order to receive healing. You have to accept the fact that you can't change what you did or what was done to you. You can only change your future by not letting it hold you back from the promise of God. It is time for a new season, a new change, but are you willing to embrace it?" He got up and said, "Thanks ma'am for the water and the food." Then he walked off. I thought to myself, "God always seems to get His message across to me." I looked up and the man was gone. He just vanished into the thin hot air.

Another week went by and it was time for me to move. I moved to 11th and Peyton Street in the west end of Little Rock. I was sitting on the porch looking for something to get into. It was a beautiful day. It was not too hot or too windy. It was just right. It was the perfect day. The kids were in the yard having a good time. My baby was happy because we had just planned her birthday party. My other two were just happy they were having another party. I heard someone whistling walking down the street and I heard, "Oh Maria!" It was Cousin Frank. We sat on the porch, laughed, and talked for a few hours. Then he left to go to work. Every time I talk to Frank about the wrongs in my life, he always had positive things to say. I made up my mind that I was going to get myself together.

I was still sitting on the porch and Tony stopped and asked me, "Did you pickup my stuff?" I said, "What are you talking about?" I told the kids it was time to come in the house. They came in and watched the Saturday cartoons.

Tony and I walked to the bedroom so Tony could try to explain his issues he had with me. I looked in Tony's eyes and I saw a blank stare in his eyes. It was like Tony's body was present but someone else was in his body. I blanked out and thought about Granny when she told me that the Devil could get into your body and take over your mind. Tony grabbed me and said, "See you are acting funny. I know you took my stuff." I said, "No, I didn't." He asked me to go out with him and I declined. He asked, "Why not?" I replied, "Because you are accusing me of stealing from you." He said, "Oh, be like that then. That nigger has you sprung out." I said, "No it's not like that." He responded, "I bet it is!" We went back and forth in conflict. Then he picked up my gun and waved the gun at me. He said, "If I find out that you are lying to me, I will kill you. You got that?" I said, "Shut the F@*k up." Before I could finish the statement, I heard, "POW!" We kept arguing. Then I felt a tense rush of air going through my body at a rapid pace. I yelled, "You shot me!" He kept quarreling. Then my body was on fire. The blood started boiling in my stomach. Next, my whole body was on fire on the inside. The pain was so great until I started sliding down the walls of my bedroom door. I went down to the floor in slow motion. There I lay on the floor and my life was passing me by at the speed of life. I saw Tony turn around, look down at me, and said, "What? What the hell? What! Oh My God! What have I done?!" Tony please go next door and see if you can use their phone and call for help. I knew that I had to stay calm because he had flipped out. He ran out the door. He was looking for someone to help me.

My little baby ran up in the room. "Momma, I heard a gunshot! We are scared!" I lay on the floor trying not to move. I knew if I moved, that bullet would move. My oldest girl said, "Momma, you are shot!" I said, "No baby, I am okay. I love you all. Go back in your room." The thought of them remembering me lying on the floor dying was heart breaking. "Momma, you have been shot. I see blood." I said, "Okay baby, yes I was shot. Please take your little sister out this room, okay? I need you to be a big sister. I love you." Tony ran back in the house and said, "The ambulance is on their way!" My baby said, "You shot my Momma!" She started crying. I asked Tony to get them out of the room. He did. I went to sleep.

I felt him slap me. He said, "Get up! They told me not to let you go to sleep." He slapped me about three times. I went back to sleep. I felt my body being moved. I woke up and all I saw was white men working on my body. I went back to sleep. I felt another bump. I woke up again to see my neighbors standing in the yard. A television camera in my face and a man from the newspaper trying to ask me questions. I wanted to talk but I went back to sleep.

I was in a dark place. I was really trying to figure out where I was but it was too dark. I felt too light to be in my old body. It was peaceful. I did not have an appetite and I was not hungry. There I was, floating in a dark room. This is peaceful. I could stay here forever. I was not sure how I was able to feel peace in a dark room. I could see in it but it was quiet as a mouse.

Then I felt that big pop. I was back on earth again. I saw a team of people working on me. Something pulled me back to the peaceful quiet room again. I stayed in the place for a while. I did not want to leave this room. It felt like I was at home.

I heard my mother's voice from the room that I was in. "Maria, don't worry about a thing. Jean will take care of your kids." I heard a second voice, "Like hell I will. You better come back and take care of your own kids. I have been more than a mother to her kids than her. It is her turn." I slipped deeper in this room. I was at peace. I saw a small bean of light coming in the quiet comfortable room that I was floating in.

Next, I felt myself being rose up into the light. I heard a soft male voice. I told him, "No, I am not going back" but my lips never moved. He understood every word that formed in my head and I understood him. I felt myself sit up and I sat with this man at the crack of the light. He said, "Look down." I looked down and I saw a team of people working on my lifeless body. Tubes were connected everywhere on my body. People were moving fast working with me.

I heard a woman say, "It is like a real circle in the waiting room. Who is this woman? The waiting room is packed. The police are turning people around. I have never saw Bloods, Crips, and Vice-lords all in one room together and they are all getting along. There was a doctor trying to come in and work on her. She has judges, lawyers, and all kinds of people in the waiting area. It looked like a circle out there. She has people fighting over who will get her kids. It is a real mess out there. We are losing her." I floated back to the dark room. My mind started focusing on my past.

I lay there thinking about every wrong thing I did. I said that I was going to apologize to everyone. My mind went into overdrive. I thought about my grandmother and the things I said to her. Mother was next on the long list. I felt bad because every time I got myself into a mess, it was her that pulled me out of the mess. I did undermine my family and myself. How could I have betrayed them like that? I did it. What kind of a monster was I? I just wanted to tell them that I was sorry for all the heartaches I caused them. My body was on fire. I am headed to hell, because of all my sins. My lifeless body just lay down. I could not move or talk. I am headed to hell at the speed of light, on a one-way ticket. My body is still slipping away to the heats of hell. Then I remember mama saying, "If you know that you are going to die, just call on the name Jesus. Call His name until you cannot say it more but make sure you ask Him to forgive you of all of your sin." I started praying, "Lord Jesus, please forgive me of my sin. I am sorry. I don't want to go to hell. Help me Lord, Jesus. Lord, I know you died on that cross for me. I am asking you to please forgive me." My mind started running back to my past. I thought about everyone who hid me when I was running from Betsy's daddy in Camden, Arkansas. I never told all of those people who helped me thank you. I just wanted to thank them for taking the time to help a hardheaded child like me. It was nice for everyone to risk their lives to save me.

I wanted to tell Uncle Hershey and Aunt Dorothy how I appreciated them for all their quick pep talks and for reminding me not to be like my mother. There were some good people in Camden that took a chance on my mother, regardless of the color of her skin. Camden was good to my family.

I thought about Aunt Daisy, and my cousin Jean. Jean had been a true backbone for my kids and me.

I thought about the Little Rock Police Department. The first responder team had helped me get through everything when I was raped. I thought about the officer that looked into my eyes and told me that he would work an extra shift just to find the person who did this to me. To that officer I just wanted to tell him thank you. That little talk with him showed me that people did care about me.

My mind was still in over drive on past mistakes. I remembered Deloris, Danielle, Tina, Joyce, Donna, Felicia and all my childhood friends. I prayed to God that I hope that I was a good friend to them. There I lay lifeless and I was still reflecting down memory lane. I thought about the first response team that was trying to save my life then. I wanted them to know that I was grateful for all of the teams that worked with me and especially Dr. Cone. Then I thought about my blood on my daddy's side. I lied there and I could not figure why they hated me so much. All I ever did was open my door for them in their time of need but I asked God to forgive me if I did something to them. I am grateful God gave me the strength to forgive the ringleader for turning them against me. Today, I want them to know that I will always love and I pray God has mercy on their soul. I tried to think as hard as I could about people that I have hurt so I could tell them that I am sorry.

Then I felt myself being pulled up again. "Pop" And there, I lay on the operator's table. I was looking up into their face. Then I heard a woman tell me it was a lot of people in the waiting room for me. She said it looked like there was a concert for me. My eyes closed and I was back in the peaceful room. I could not think of nothing in the world but to lay there forever.

I heard that man's soft voice again say, "Come." I was floating up again. I met him at the crack of the light. I automatically knew to look down. I saw my oldest daughter rubbing my arms. She was trying not to touch the tubes that were hanging out my arm. She asked her Granny, "Who is going to cook for us?" Momma replied, "I guess Jean." I asked the man if I could go back. I tried to ask him as nice as I could. Then I tried to reason with him. My gut told me not to make this man mad. Then, I felt myself falling. Back to the darkness, the light that I once sat in was disappearing to the darkness. I kept feeling myself fall deeper and deeper into the darkness. I just laid there in the complete darkness. I knew I was at end of my journey.

I heard the man say look at this. I looked down the tunnel where the light was coming from the room. I asked the man was that me. He didn't stay a word. He just stared down dark the tunnel where the light was coming from. The bright room started moving closer to us. My vision became brighter. I heard Momma's voice preaching to different people on the bus. There the man and I stared at myself while listening to Momma teach different things on the Greyhound bus. He looked at Momma with pride. He was pleased with her.

God has brought me a long way and I am not turning back now. I am too blessed to be stressed.

I am glad God feels my pains. When one door shuts, two more doors open. That is why I order my steps in the Lord… Psalms 124:2. If it had not been the Lord who was on our side, when men rose up against us they would shallow me up.

Father God today I am going to trust you because you are faithful and trustworthy. I am making a commitment to trust in you (Father God) with all my heart and lean not on my own understanding. In all my ways, I acknowledge you, and you (Father God) will make my paths straight. I am blessed. For all I trust in the Lord, in whom is my confidence.

I felt my body floating back to the dark place again. I could not move or talk. The man was gone. I was there all alone in the peace and quietness.

Summary
GOD IS STILL IN CONTROL IN THE END

It is not the most comfortable sensation in the world, but tension is not always a bad thing—in fact, it can often bring out the best in you. A stressful situation can give you creativity and intelligent terrifically satisfying jolt. So stop seeking out people who are completely compatible with you. If you surround yourself with only like-minded thinkers, your own mind and soul will no longer be challenged—and they will no longer grow.

Isaiah 58:11. The Lord will guide you continually, satisfy your soul in drought, and strengthen your bones; you shall be like a watered garden, and like a spring of water, whose waters do not fail. God open up the windows of Heaven and touch every one of us today. Lord bless my family and my friends. Touch us right now Lord. I pray in your name. Jesus Christ. AMEN.

7.Ask, and it shall be given you; seek and ye shall find; knock; and it shall be opened unto you; 8. For every one that asketh receiveth; he that seeketh findeth; and to him that knocketh it shall be opened. 9. Or what man is there of you, whom if his son ask bread, will he give him a stone? 10. Or if he asks a fish, will he give him a serpent? 11. If ye then, being evil, know how to give good gifts unto your children, how much more shall your Father which is in heaven give food things to them that ask him? My prayer today is: Lord help us to be good food giver. So when we seek we find. So when we knock doors will be open. Help us Lord. Please help us right now.In your name Jesus Christ name.. I pray.. AMEN

Section 2

Momma's 911 Closet Prayers

Nighttime Prayer

I PLEAD THE blood of Jesus onto my life as I lay down to sleep. I plead the blood over me and my family life, our house, health, and strength. I pray that you keep us safe. I pray that we get the rest that we need. Thank you for keeping us safe. Thank you for keeping your angels all around us to keep us safe. Amen

Food Time Prayer

God is good. God is great. Let us thank Him for our food. LORD please blerss our food. Let our soul be fed as well as our bodies. Bless the people who prepared this food. Thank you Lord. Amen

God Does Hear Your Prayers

John 14: 1. Let not your heart be troubled; ye believe in God, believe also in me. 2. In my Father's house are many mansions: if it were not so, I would have told you. I go prepare a place. 11. Believe me that I am in the Father.

Entering in the Closet Prayers

Prayer for Weakness

God understands that we are weak. He knows that we are sinners. All He wants is for us to admit that we need Him. Admit that we are helpless without Him.

2 Timothy 4:14–18, 22

14. Alexander, the coppersmith, (put your enemies, or your problem in here) did me much evil: the Lord reward him according to his works; 15. Of whom be thou ware also for he hath greatly withstood our words. 16. At first, my answer no man stood with me but all men forsook me: I pray God that it may not be laid to their charge. 17. Notwithstanding the Lord stood with me, and strengthened me; that by me the preaching might be fully known, and that all the Gentiles might hear: and I was delivered out of the mouth

of the lion. 18. And the Lord shall deliver me from every evil work, and will preserve me unto his heavenly kingdom: to whom be glory forever and ever. Amen.

22. The Lord Jesus Christ be with thy spirit. Grace is with you. Amen.

Hebrews 4:12–16

12. For the word of God is quick, and powerful, and shaper than any two edged sword, piercing even to the dividing asunder of soul and spirit, and of the joints and marrow, and is a discerner of the thoughts and intents of the heart. 13. Neither is there any creature that is not manifest in his sight: but all things are naked and opened unto the eyes of him with whom we have to do. 14. Seeing then that we have a great high priest, that is passed into the heavens, Jesus the Son of God, let us hold fast our profession. 15. For we have not an high priest which cannot be touched with the feeling of our infirmities; but was in all points tempted like as we are, yet without sin. 16. Let us therefore come boldly unto the throne of grace that we may obtain mercy, and find grace to help, in time of need.

He understands what we are going through. He has already been through what you are going through. He can see far down the road.

He is just preparing us for his next purposes. Just have a little faith in him. He knows it is hard to hold your faith at times. He loves us. He will be there for you when no one else will. He is waiting to hear from you. His ear is always open for you, which shows that this is true love.

Ephesians 6:22–24

22. Whom I have sent unto you for the same purpose, that ye might know our affairs, and that he might comfort your heart. 23. Peace be to the brethren, and love with faith, from God the Father and the Lord Jesus Christ. 24. Grace is with all of them that love our Lord Jesus Christ in sincerity. Amen.

Hebrews 6:1–7

1. Therefore leaving the principles of the doctrine of Christ, let us go on unto perfection; not laying again the foundation of repentance from dead works, and of faith toward God. 2. Of the doctrine of baptisms, and laying on the hands, and of resurrection of the dead, and eternal judgment. 3. And this will we do, if God permit. 4. For it is impossible for those who were once enlightened, and have tasted of the heavenly gift, and were made partakers of the Holt Ghost. 5. And have tasted the good word of God, and

the powers of the world to come. 6. If they shall fall away, to renew them again unto repentance, seeing they crucify to themselves the Son of God afresh, and put him to an open shame. 7. For the earth, this drinketh in the rain that cometh upon it, and bringeth forth herbs. Meet for them by whom it is dressed, receiveth blessing from God.

Prayer for Peace

Isaiah 60:1–11

1. Arise, shine; for thy light is come, and the glory of the Lord is risen upon thee. 2. For, behold, the darkness shall cover the earth, and gross darkness the people; but the Lord shall rise upon thee, and his glory shall be seen upon thee. 3. And the Gentiles shall come to thy light, and kings to the brightness of thy rising. 4. Lift up thine eyes round about, and see all they gather themselves together, they come to thee; thy sons shall come from far, and thy daughters shall be nursed at thy side. 5. Then thou shall see, and flow together, and thine heart shall fear, and enlarged; because the abundance of the sea shall be converted unto thee, the forces of the Gentiles shall come unto thee. 6. The multitude of camels shall cover thee, the dromedaries of Midian and Ephah; all they shall bring gold and incense; and they shall shew forth the praises of the Lord. 7. All

the flocks of Kedar shall be gathered together unto thee, the rams of Nebaioth shall minister unto thee: they shall come up with acceptance on mine altar and the will glorify the house on my glory. 8. Who are these that fly as a cloud and as the doves to their windows? 9. Surely the isles shall wait for me, and the ships of Tarshish first, to bring thy sons from far, their silver and their gold with them unto the name of the Lord thy God, and to the Holy One of Israel, because he hath glorified thee. 10. And the sons of strangers shall build up thy walls, and their kings shall minister unto thee; for in my wrath I will smote thee, but in my favor have I had mercy on thee. 11. Therefore thy gates shall be open continually; they shall not be shut day or nor night; that men may bring unto thee the forces of the Gentiles, and that their kings may be brought.

Isaiah 61

1. The spirit of the Lord God is upon me; because the Lord hath anointed me to preach good tidings unto the meek; he hath sent me to blind up the brokenhearted, to proclaim liberty to the captives, and the opening of the prison to them that are bound; 2. To proclaim the acceptable year of the Lord, and the day of vengeance of our God; to comfort all that mourn; 3. To appoint unto them that mourn in Zion, to give unto them beauty for ashes, the oil of joy

for mourning, the garment of praise for the spirit of heaviness; that they might be called trees of righteousness, the planting of the Lord, that he might be glorified. 4. And they shall build the old wastes, they shall raise up the former desolations, and they shall repair the waste cities, the desolations of many generations. 5. And strangers shall stand and feed your flocks, and the sons of the alien shall be your plowmen and your vinedressers. 7. For your shame ye shall have double; and for confusion they shall rejoice in their portion: therefore in their land they shall possess the double: everlasting joy shall be unto them. 8. For I the Lord love judgment, I hate robbery for burnt offering; and I will direct their work in truth, and I will make an everlasting covenant with them. 9. And their seed shall be known among the Gentiles, and their offspring among the people; all that see them shall acknowledge them, that they are the seed, which the Lord hath blessed. 10. I will greatly rejoice in the Lord, my soul shall be joyful in my God; for he hath clothed me with the garments of salvation, he hath covered me with the robe of righteousness, as a bridegroom decketh himself with ornaments, and as a bride adorneth herself with her jewels. 11. For as the earth bringeth forth her bud, and as the garden causeth the things that are sown in it to spring forth; so the Lord God will cause righteousness and praise to spring forth before all the nations.

Keeping your faith in God and He will give you the rest.

Prayer for Redemptions

Ephesians 1:7

In Him we have redemption through his blood, the forgiveness of our sins, according to the riches of His grace. 8. Which He made to abound towards us in all wisdom and prudence 9. Having made know to us the mystery of His will, according to His good pleasure, which He purposed in Himself

Isaiah 63:14–16

14. As a beast goeth down into the valley, the Spirit of the Lord caused him to rest; so didst thou lead thy people, to make thyself a glorious name. 15. Look down from heaven, and behold from the habitation of thy holiness and thy glory; where is thy zeal thy strength, the sounding of thy bowels and of thy mercies toward me? Are they restrained? 16. Doubtless thou art our father, though Abraham is ignorant of us, and Israel acknowledges us not: thou, O Lord, art our father, our redeemer; thy name is from everlasting.

Once you asked God to forgive you, he does and He wipes away all of your sins. The hardest thing for me is to do forgive myself. This is what stopped me from moving forward.

Today I am praying that God helps me not to sin and to help me to be able to forgive myself so that I can move forward, and not stand still in the same place. God whoever prayed this prayer with me. Touch us Lord. Guide us. In your name, we pray. Amen.

Psalm 1:1–3

1. Blessed is the man that walketh not in the counsel of the ungodly, nor standeth in the way of sinners, nor sitteth in the seat of the scornful. 2. But his delight is in the law doth he meditate day and night. 3. And he shall be like a tree planted by the rivers of the water, that bringeth forth in his season; his leaf also shall not wither; and whatsoever he doeth shall prosper.

Psalm 3:3–5

3. But thou, O Lord, art a shield for me; my glory, and the lifter up of mine head. 4. I cried unto the Lord with my voice, and he heard me out of his holy hill. Selah. 5. I laid me down and slept; I awaked; for the Lord sustained me.

Psalm 4:7–8

7. Thou hast put gladness in my heart, more than in the time that their corn and their wine increased. 8. I will both lay me down in peace, and sleep: for thou, Lord, only makest me dwell in safety.

Psalm 37:7

7. Rest in the Lord, and wait patiently for him who prospereth in his way, because of the man who bringeth wicked devices to pass.

Have patience and wait on the Lord and he will give you rest.

Psalm 23

1. The Lord is my shepherd; I shall not want. 2. He maketh me to lie down in green pastures; he leadeth beside the still waters 3. Restoreth my soul; he leadeth me in the paths of righteousness for his name's sake. 4. Yea, though I walk through the valley of the shadow of death, I will fear no evil: for thou art with thy rod; thy staff thy comfort me.5. Thou prepares a table before me in the presence of my enemies; thou anointest my head with oil; my cup runneth

over. 6. Surely goodness and mercy shall follow me all the days of my life: and I will dwell in the house of the Lord forever. Amen.

Psalm 100

1. Make a joyful noise unto the Lord, all ye lands. 2. Serve the Lord with gladness; come before his presence with singing. 3. Know ye that the Lord he is God; it is he that hath made us, and not we ourselves; we are his people, and the sheep of his pasture. 4. Enter into his gates with thanksgiving, and into his courts with praise; be thankful unto him, and bless his name. 5. For the Lord is good; his mercy is everlasting; and his truth endureth to all generations.

Enemies

Psalm 102

1. Hear my prayer, O Lord, and let my cry come unto thee, 2. Hide not thy face from me in the day when I am in trouble; incline thine ear unto me; in the day when I call answer me speedily. 3. For my days are consumed like smoke, and my bones are burned as an hearth. 4. My heart is smitten, and withered like grass; so that I forget to eat my bread. 5. By reason of the voice of my groaning my bones cleave to

my skin. 6. I am like a pelican of the wilderness: I am like an owl of the desert. 7. I watch, and am as a sparrow alone upon the housetop. 8. Mine enemies reproach me all the day; and they that are mad against me are sworn against me. 9. For I have eaten ashes like bread, mingled my drink with weeping, 10. Because of thine indignation and thy wrath; for thou hast lifted me up, and cast me down. 11. My days are like a shadow that declineth; and I am withered like grass. 12. But thou, O Lord, shall endure forever; and thy remembrance unto all generations. 13. Thou shalt arise, and have mercy upon Zion, for the time to favor her, yea, the set time, is come. 14. For thy servants take pleasure in her stones, and favor the dust thereof. 15. So the heathen shall fear the name of the Lord and all the kings of the earth thy glory. 16. When the Lord shall build up Zion, he shall appear in his glory. 17. He will regard the prayer of the destitute, and not despise their prayer. 18. This shall be written for the generation to come: and the people who shall be created shall praise the Lord. 19. For he hath looked down from the height of his sanctuary; from heaven did the Lord behold the earth; 20. To hear the groaning of the prisoner; to lose those that are appointed to death; 21. To declare the name of the Lord in Zion, and his praise in Jerusalem; 22. When the people are gathered together, and the kingdoms, to serve the Lord.

Psalm 109:1–7

1. Hold not thy peace, O God of my praise; 2. For the mouth of the wicked and the mouth of the deceitful are opened against me: they have spoken against me with a lying tongue. 3. They compassed me about also with words of hatred; and fought against me without a cause. 4. For my love they are my adversaries: but I give myself unto prayer. 5. And they have rewarded me evil for good, hatred for my love. 6. Set thou a wicked man over him: and let Satan stand at his right hand. 7. When he shall be judged, let him be condemned: and let his prayers become sin.

Psalm 110

1. The Lord said unto my Lord, Sit thou at my right hand, until I make thine enemies thy footstool. 2. The Lord shall send the rod of thy strength out of Zion: rule thou in the midst of thine enemies. 3. Thy people shall be willing in the day of thy power, in the beauties of holiness from the womb of the morning: thou hast the dew of thy youth. 4. The Lord hath sworn, and will not repent, Thou art a priest for ever after the order of Melchizedek. 5. The Lord at thy right hand shall strike through kings in the day of his wrath. 6. He shall judge among the heathen, he shall fill the places

with the dead bodies; he shall wound the heads over many countries. 7. He shall therefore he lift up the head.

Psalm 116

1. I love the Lord, because he hath heard my voice and my supplications. 2. Because he hath inclined his ear unto me, therefore will I call upon him as long as I live. 3. The sorrows of death compassed me, and the pains of hell gat hold upon me: I found trouble and sorrow. (Think about what is bothering you, so God can fix it.) 4. Then called I upon the name of the Lord; O Lord, I beseech thee, deliver my soul. 5. Gracious is the Lord, and righteous; yea, our God is merciful. 6. The Lord preserveth the simple; I was brought low, and he helped me. 7. Return unto thy, O rest my soul; for the Lord hath dealt bountifully with thee. 8. For thou hast delivered my soul from death, mines eyes from tears, and my feet from falling. 9. I will walk before the Lord in the land of the living. 10. I believed, therefore have I spoken; I was greatly afflicted: 11. I said in my haste, All men are liars. 12. What shall I render unto the Lord for all his benefits toward me? 13. I will take the cup of salvation, and call upon the name of the Lord. 14. I will pay my vows unto the Lord now in the presence of all his people. 15. Precious in the sight of the Lord is the death of his saints. 16. O Lord, truly I am thy servant; I am thy

servant, and the son of thine handmaid: thou hast loosed my bonds. 17. I will offer to thee sacrifice of thanksgiving, and will call upon the name of the Lord. 18. I will pay my vows unto the Lord now in the presence of all his people. 19. In the courts of the Lord's house, in the midst of thee, O Jerusalem. Praise.

Psalm 117

1. O Praise the Lord, all ye nations: praise him, all ye people. 2. For his merciful kindness is great toward us: and the truth of the Lord endureth for. Praise ye the Lord. Amen.

Psalm 91:15

15. When they call on me, I will answer; I will be with them in trouble. I will rescue and honor them.

Comfort

Isaiah 40:1–2

Comfort, yes, comfort my people! Say your God. 2. Speak comfort to Jerusalem, and cry out to her, that her welfare is ended, that her iniquity is pardoned; for she has received from the Lord's hands double for all her sins.

Matthew 5:3–4

3. Blessed are the poor in spirit, for theirs is the kingdom of heaven. 4. Blessed are those who mourn, for they shall be comforted.

Isaiah 40:1–5

1. Comfort ye, comfort ye my people, saith your God. 2. Speak ye comfortably to Jerusalem, and cry unto her, that her warfare is accomplished, that her iniquity is pardon: for she hath received of the Lord's hand double for all her sins. 3. The voice of him that crieth in the wilderness, Prepare ye the way of the Lord, make straight in the desert a highway for our God. 4. Every valley shall be exalted, and every mountain and hill shall be made low: and the crooked shall be made straight and the rough places plain: 5. And the glory of the Lord shall be revealed, and all fresh shall see it together; for the mouth of the Lord hath spoken it.

Building Real Relationships

Mutual respect is at the very core of any successful relationship. Be alert. Doing the right thing sometimes requires the courage to face down any fear.

What part do you play in the relationship, (A or B)?

(A) Are you the one who builds the relationship?
(B) Are you the one who is demolishing the relationship away?

Finding a Mate

My inbox is full of people asking me to pray for them for a mate. If that is your desire, I encourage you to ask the

Lord to prepare you for marriage. Submit to God's future plans for your life, and purpose to please Him. Do not make your deliberations, without knowing His will, at the expense of your personal spiritual growth and transformation. Going from glory to glory is not dependent on having a spouse.

Prayer

Father, I come before you in the name of Jesus, asking for your will to be done in my life as I look to you for a marriage partner. I submit to the constant ministry of transformation by the Holy Spirit, making my petition known to you. Prepare me for marriage by bringing everything to light that has been hidden wounded–emotions, walls of denial, emotional isolation, silence or excessive talking, anger, or rigidity [name any walls that separates you from healthy relationships and anything that separates you from God's love and grace]. The weapons of my warfare are not carnal but mighty through you. I lay aside every weight, and the sins, which so easily ensure me. I will run with endurance because there is race that is set before me, looking unto Jesus, the author and finisher of my faith. I come before you, Father, expressing my desire for a Christian mate. I petition that yours will be done in my life. Now I enter into that blessed rest by adhering to, trusting in, and relying on you. In Jesus name, Amen.

Isaiah: 62

1: For Zion's sake will I not hold my peace, and for Jerusalem's sake I will not rest, until the righteousness therefore go forth as brightness, and the salvation therefore as a lamp that burneth. 2. And the Gentiles shall see thy righteousness, and all kings thy glory: and thou shalt be called by a new name, which the mouth of the Lord shall name. 3. Thou shalt also be crown of glory in the hand of the Lord, and a royal diadem in the hand of thy God. 4. Thou shalt no more be termed Forsaken; neither shall thy land any more is termed desolated: but thou shalt be called Hephzibah, and thy land Beulah: for the Lord delighted in thee, and thy land shall be married. 5. For as a young man marrieth a virgin, so shall thy sons marry thee: and as the bridegroom rejoiceth over the bride, so shall thy God rejoice over thee. 6. I have set guards upon thy walls, O Jerusalem, which shall never hold their peace day nor night: ye that make mention of the Lord, keep not silence. 7. And give him no rest, till established, and till he make Jerusalem a praise in the earth. 8. The Lord hath sworn by his right hand, and by the arm of his strength; Surely I will no more give thy corn to be meat for thine enemies; and the sons of the stranger shall not drink thy wine, for the which thou hast laboreth: 9. But they that have gathered it shall eat it, and praise the Lord; and they that brought it together shall drink it in courts of my holiness. 10. Go through, go through the gates; prepare ye the way of the people; cast up, cast up the highway; gather out the stones; lift up a standard for the people. 11. Behold, the Lord hath proclaimed unto the end of the world, Say yes to the daughter of Zion, Behold, thy salvation cometh; behold, his reward is with him, and his work before him. 12. And they shall call them, the holy people, The redeemed of the Lord: and thou shall be called, Sought out, A city not forsaken. Amen.

Isaiah 61:10–11

10. I will greatly rejoice in the Lord, my soul shall be joyful in my God; for he hath clothed me with the garments of salvation, he hath covered me with the robe of righteousness, as a bridegroom decketh himself with ornaments, and as a bride adornedeth herself with her jewels. 11. For as the earth bringeth forth her bud, and as the garden causeth the things are sown in it to spring forth; so the Lord God will cause righteousness and praise to spring forth before all the nations.

Isaiah 40:25, 26

25. To whom then will ye liken me, or shall I be equal? Said the Holy Ones.

God is ALWAYS by your side. He loves you that much.

Trials and Tribulations

Sometimes we all have some sort of weakness in our lives and we need to be delivered from our problems. Our flesh is weak and we are helpless when we try to fight our problems alone. The last thing we want is a person talking to you about what your problem is. Then they point their finger at you in your time of need. Majority of the time, we already know what the problem is. We need help in finding a solution: Mark 1 tells us about our flesh being possessed with the devil. People always want to blame things on the devil. However, the book of Matthew and Mark talk about the amazing work that our God did. How he went to town casting out demons. So why is it so hard today to believe that the demon still exists? I do not understand people (Churchgoers or sometimes Christians) and the way they use God (when it is convenient). When it is going good, everyone wants to play a part in your life. This not the way God designs Christians or His church house. See, Christians are able to heal mentally sick people and the church is the hospital where mentally sick people go. Sick people are people who are possessed with the devil and full of sin.

Mark 10:27

Humanly speaking, it is impossible. But, not with God. Everything is possible with God.

He gives power to the weak ones

Isaiah 40:29

He gives power to the weak and strength to the powerless.

Mark 1:10

10. And straightway coming up out of the water, he saw the heavens opened, and the Spirit like a dove descending upon him; 11. And there came a voice from heaven, saying, Thou art my beloved Son, in whom I am well pleased. 12. And immediately the spirit driveth him unto the wilderness. 13. And he was there in the wildness forty days, tempted of the Satin; and with the wild beasts; and the angels ministered unto him. 14. Now after that John was put in prison, Jesus

came into Galilee, preaching the gospel of the kingdom of God. 15. And saying, "The time is fulfilled, and the kingdom of God is at hand; repent ye and believe the gospel."

It is always a reason as to why things happen the way it happens. Jesus does understand what you are going through. Its part of His plan and the way He prunes us. Have faith, be patient, and wait.

He does give a way of cleaning you up to where no one can tell what you have gone through. Do not worry about what your family or associates think about you. Remember that God has the final word and His way is best for you. In the end, you should give him the glory.

Mark 1:24–27

24. Saying let us alone; what have we to do with thee. Thou Jesus of Nazareth? Art who thou destroy us? I know thee who thou art, the Holy One of God. 25. And Jesus rebuked him, saying, "Hold thy peace, and come out of him." 26. And when the unclean spirit had torn him, and cried with a loud voice, he came out of him. 27. And they were all amazed, in so much that they questioned, among themselves, saying, what new doctrine is this? For with authority commandeth he even the unclean spirits, and they do obey him. God is good. Words cannot say enough about him.

My God Can Heal Anyone

I understand what it feels like to be imprisoned, or to be trapped inside my mind and body. I know what it is like to have an addiction so strong and powerful until it controls your every thought. I also know what it is like to be handicapped where you have to wait on someone to help you go to the bathroom or to have someone feed you because you cannot feed yourself. It is stressful and hard having to need someone to help you with your daily needs.

People take daily living for granted. I want you to know that I thank my God for my recovery. I give him all the praise and honor that is due. If it was not for the goodness of him, I would have been dead and gone. I would have lost my mind. I love him. I need him in my life. I can truly say that I am honestly nothing without him.

Mark 1:

41. And Jesus, moved with compassion, put forth his hand, touched him, and saith unto him, "I will; clean." 42. And soon as he had spoken, immediately the leprosy departed from him, and he was cleansed.

I was just a sinner who was lost in this world caught up in all kinds of sins. I used to smoke and drink in hopes that when I woke up from my high that all of my problems would be gone. When I came down from my high, my problems had just gotten bigger. The things that I had were headaches, stomachaches, pride aches, and money aches. To top it all off I was still nothing but a lost soul who still needed a lot of help. God healed me from my addiction to drugs, alcohol, cigarettes, and he restored my health and strength. He brought me back from the dead. He is my all. I give him all the praise and honor that is past due.

God Gives Power to the Weak

2 Corinthians 12:9

My grace is all you need. My power works best in weakness.

Psalm 86:9

All the nations you made will come and bow before you; Lord, they will praise your holy name.

Psalm 93:4

Mightier than the violent raging of the seas, mightier that the breakers on the shore-the Lord above is mightier that these!

Psalm 46

1. God is refuge and strength, a present help in trouble. 2. Therefore will not we fear, though the earth be removed, and though the mountains be carried into the midst of the sea; 3. Though the waters thereof roar and be troubled, though the mountains shake with the swelling thereof. 4. There is a river, the streams whereof shall make glad the city of God, the holy place of the tabernacles of the most High. 5. God is in the midst of her; she shall not be moved; God shall help her and that right early. 6. The heathen raged, the kingdoms were moved: he uttered his voice, the earth melted. 7. The Lord of hosts is with us; the God of Jacob is our refuge. Selah. 8. Come, behold the works of the Lord, what desolations he hath made the earth. 9. He maketh wars to cease unto the end of the earth: he breaketh the bow, and cutteth the spear in sunder; he burneth the chariot in the fire. 10. Be still, and know that I am God; I will be exalted among the heathen, I will be exalted in the earth, 11. The Lord of host is with us; the God of Jacob is our refuge. Selah

Mark 2:14–17

14. And as he passed by, he saw Levi the son of Alpheus sitting at the receipt of custom, and said unto him, "Follow me." And he arose and followed him. 15. And it came to pass, that, as Jesus sat at meat in the house, many publicans and sinners sat also together with Jesus and his disciples; for there were many, and they followed him. 16. And when the scribes and Pharisees saw him eat with publicans and sinners, they said unto his disciples. How is it that he eateth and drinketh with publicans and sinners? 17. When Jesus heard it, he saith unto them, "They that are whole have no need of the physician, but they that are sick: I came not to call the righteous, but sinners to repentance."

Mark 3:10–11

10. For he had healed many; insomuch that they pressed upon him for to touch him, as many as had plagues. 11. And unclean spirits, when they saw him, fell down before him, and cried, saying, Thou art the Son of God.

Mark 22:–29

22. And the scribes who came down from Jerusalem said, He hath Beelzebub, and by the prince of the devils casteth he out devils. 23. And he called them unto him, and said unto them in parables, "How can Satan cast out Satan? 24. And if a kingdom be divided against itself, that kingdom cannot stand. 26. And if Satan rises up against himself, and

be divided, he cannot stand, but hath an end. 27. No man can enter into a strong man's house, and spoil his goods, except he will first bind the strong man; and then he will spoil his house. 28. Verily I say unto you, all sins shall be forgiven unto the sons of men, and blasphemies wherewith so ever they shall blaspheme; 29. But he that shall blaspheme against the Holy Ghost hath never forgiveness, but is in danger of eternal damnation."

Mark 2:5–12

5. When Jesus saw their faith, he said unto the sick of the palsy, "Son, thy sins be forgiven thee." 6. But there were certain of the scribes sitting there, and reasoning in their hearts. 7. Why doth this man thus speak blasphemies? Who can forgive sins but God only? 8. And immediately when Jesus perceived in his spirit that they so reasoned, within themselves, he said unto them, "Why reason ye these things in your heart? 9. Whether is it easier to say to the sick of the palsy, Thy sins be forgiven thee; or to say, Arise, and take up thy bed, and walk? 10. But that ye may know that the Son of man hath power on earth to forgive sins. (He saith to the sick of the palsy,) 11. I say unto thee, Arise, and take up thy bed, go thy way into thine house." 12. And immediately he rose, took up the bed, and went forth before them all; inso-

much that they were all amazed and glorified God, saying, we never saw it on this fashion.

God's Food

You would be surprised how many of your neighbors next door to you, who do not have food in their house. Millions of American families do not have food to feed their kids.

Most of them will not tell you because they know that you will tell someone and then someone will tell someone else. You have to put yourself in others shoes. Would you want everyone one to know that you do not have food in your house?

We like to look good. We like everyone to know that we are ballers…you know, the real shot callers. What do you think that does to the person who does not have anything? They are already at their lowest point. They do not need everyone else to know it.

I remember a day we did not have food. We had one more day until Momma got paid. She knew that God would show, so she said, "Let sit down and bless this table." My Granny said, "What are you doing? Do you see any food on this table?" She said, "Juanita I have saw you do a lot of things, but this takes the cake."

Momma never cared about what a person thought of her so she kept on praying.

Isaiah 55:1

1. Ho! Everyone who thirsts, Come to the waters; and you who have no money, Come, buy and eat. Yes, come; buy wine and milk without money and without price.

John 4:33–38

33. Therefore the disciples said to one another, "Has anyone brought Him anything to eat?" 34. Jesus said to them, "My food is to do the will of Him who sent me, and to finish His work. 35. "Do you not say, "There are still four months and then comes the harvest"? Behold, I say to you, lift up your eyes and look at the fields, for they are already white for harvest! 36. "And he who reaps receives wages, and gathers fruit for eternal life, that both he who sows and he who reaps may rejoices together, 37. "For in this saying is true; One sows and another reaps" 38. "I sent you to reap that for which you have not labored; others have labored, and you have entered into labors."

Isaiah 58:9–11

9. Then you shall call, and the Lord will answer; you shall cry, and He will say, "Here I am" "If you take away the yoke

from your midst, the pointing of the finger, and speaking wickedness, 10. If you extend your soul to the hungry and satisfy the afflicted soul, then your light shall dawn in the darkness, and darkness shall be as the noonday. 11. The Lord will guide you continually, and satisfy your soul in drought, and strengthen your bones; you shall be like a watered garden, and like spring of water, whose waters do not fail.

Isaiah:55

1. Ho every one that thirsteth, come, ye to the waters, and he that hath no money; come ye, buy, and eat; yea, come buy wine and milk without money and without price.

Matthew 6:33

33. Seek the kingdom of God above All else, and live righteously, and he will give you everything you need.

Luke 6:38

Give and you will receive. Your gift will return to you in full-pressed down, shaken together to make room for more, running over, and poured into your lap. The amount you give will determine the amount you get back.

Malachi 3:8–11

8. Will a man rob God? Yet ye have robbed me. But ye say, Wherein have we robbed thee? In tithes and offerings. 9. Ye are cursed with a curse: for ye have robbed me, even these whole nations. 10. Bring ye all the tithes into the storehouse, that there may be meat in mine house, and prove me now herewith, saith the Lord of hosts, if I will not open you the windows of heaven, and pour you out a blessing, that there shall not be room enough to receive it. 11. And I will rebuke the devourer for your sakes, and he shall not destroy fruits of your ground; neither shall your vine cast her fruit before the time in the field, saith the Lord of hosts.

Proverbs 23:4–5

Do not wear yourself out trying to get rich. Be wise enough to know to quit. In the blink of an eye, wealth disappears, for it will sprout wings and fly away like an eagle.

Matthew 6:19–21

Do not store up treasures here on earth, where moths eat them and rust destroys them, and where thieves break in and steal. Store your treasures in heaven, where moths and rust cannot destroy, and thieves do not break in and steal.

Wherever your treasure is, there the desires of your heart will also be.

Ephesians 3:8

8. To me, who are less than the least of all the saints, this grace was given, that I should preach among the Gentiles the unsearchable riches of Christ.

Ephesians 3:8–21

8. To me, who are less than the least of all the saints, this grace was given, that I should preach among the Gentiles the unsearchable riches of Christ, 9. and to make all see what is the fellowship of the mystery, which from the beginning of the ages has been hidden in God who created all things through Jesus Christ; 10. To the intent that now the manifold wisdom of God might be made known by the truth church to the principalities and powers in the heavenly places, 11. According to eternal purpose which He accomplished in Christ Jesus our Lord. 12 in whom we have boldness and access with confidence through faith in Him 13. Therefore, I asked that you do not lose heart at my tribulations for you, which is glory. 14. For this reason I bow my knees to the Father of Lord Jesus Christ, 15. From whom the whole family in heaven and earth is named, 16

that He would grant you, according to the riches of His glory, to be strengthened with might through His Spirit in the inner man, 17. That Christ may dwell in your hearts through faith; that you, being rooted and grounded in love, 18. May be able to comprehend with all the saints what is the width and length and depth and height–19. To know the love of Christ this passed knowledge; that you may be filled with all the fullness of God. 20. Now to Him who is able to do exceedingly above all that we ask or think, according to the power that works in us, 21. To Him be glory in the church by Christ Jesus to all generations, forever and ever, Amen.

John 16:5–12

Suggested further reading: Genesis 50:15–20

Our Lord's words seem to convey a reproof to the disciples for not enquiring more earnestly about the heavenly home to which their Master was going. Peter, no doubt, had said with vague curiosity, "Whither goest thou?" (John 13:36); but his question had not originated in a desire to know the place, so much as in surprise that his Lord was going at all. Our Lord seems here to say, "If your hearts were in a right frame, you would seek to understand the nature of my going and the place to which I go."